# Orwashers
### NEW YORK'S ORIGINAL ARTISAN BAKERY

# ARTISAN BREAD

![Orwashers logo] Orwashers
NEW YORK'S ORIGINAL ARTISAN BAKERY

# ARTISAN BREAD

## 100 YEARS OF TECHNIQUES AND RECIPES

Race Point
PUBLISHING

**Race Point**
PUBLISHING

An imprint of Quayside Publishing Group, Inc.
276 Fifth Avenue, Suite 206
New York, New York 10001

RACE POINT PUBLISHING and the distinctive Race Point Publishing logo
are trademarks of the Quayside Publishing Group, Inc.

This 2014 edition published by Race Point Publishing
by arrangement with The Book Shop, Ltd.

EDITOR Susan Sulich
DESIGNER Tim Palin Creative

PHOTO CREDITS
**Josh Shaub:** Covers, 3, 8, 13, 21, 24, 27, 28-33, 59, 70 (left), 71, 90-92, 95, 97, 114, 116-117, 119, 120, 123, 125, 126, 129, 131, 132, 135, 137, 138, 141, 142, 145, 147, 148, 151, 152, 154-155, 157, 158, 160-161, 163, 164, 167, 169, 171, 172, 175, 180, 183, 184, 187, 188, 191, 192, 195, 199, 206, 208, 213; **Thinkstock:** 5, 34, 36, 37, 39, 40, 44-45, 46, 48, 51, 75, 80, 83, 84, 86, 88, 102, 178; **Grant Delin/Good Eggs:** 6-7, 11, 14, 16, 19, 22, 23, 38, 52-57, 76-77, 78; **Shutterstock:** Woodgrain background throughout; **Josh Hoffman:** 47, 58, 60-65, 67-69, 70 (right), 105, 108-112, 201, 215 (top left, top right, bottom left); **Getty:** 73, 202, 204, 205, 215 (bottom right); **Courtesy of Keith Cohen:** 98-99, 174, 196, 200, 203, 204 (bottom), 211; **Courtesy of North Country Mills:** 100; **Courtesy of Channing Daughters:** 179; **Courtesy of Sixpoint Brewery:** 181

ISBN-13: 978-1-937994-42-6

Printed in China

2 4 6 8 10 9 7 5 3 1

www.racepointpub.com

# CONTENTS

"*Good bread is the most fundamentally satisfying of all foods;
and good bread with fresh butter the greatest of feasts.*"

-James Beard

# INTRODUCTION

When I taste a loaf of freshly baked bread, I sometimes think about how this humble and commonplace item on the dinner table has been such a prodigious part of our world for centuries, shaping not only our bodies, but also our cultures. Over the years bread has symbolized many things to many people: It has been a means of survival, a purveyor of comfort, an ambassador of peace, and the embodiment of heritage and tradition.

I often wonder, did I choose bread, or did bread choose me? I'm not really sure. Like many college graduates before me, I was uncertain of what path I would take. In school I worked as a line cook, which sparked my interest in the culinary world. In need of a job, I began to wait tables in New York's Brooklyn Heights to pay the bills while I figured out what to do next. As luck would have it, I knew someone at an employment agency who felt I would be a good fit for a sales job at a small, artisanal wholesale bakery in Manhattan. One day in 1994, I went in for an interview and was hired on the spot. That job was my first and last job working for someone else. I stayed there for fourteen years, learning all facets of the business. I worked in sales, product development, quality control, operations—you name it, I did it! When there was a blizzard, I was the person outside digging snow out from under the trucks that were buried in the mounds, to make sure the deliveries were made. In order to help boost sales, I began to get more involved in the production side of the business.

A successful business must have happy customers. Customers are happy when there's a quality product. I began noticing there were some quality control issues, so I worked with the production team to troubleshoot these. I discovered that small changes can make a big difference, and this part of the job thrilled me. Troubleshooting comes naturally to me because I'm an analytical person. I quickly began to see patterns that could help us improve the bread and create a more consistent product.

After fourteen years, the direction of the bakery shifted, and I was faced with the decision to either join another artisanal bakery or venture out on my own. I heard through word of mouth that Orwashers Bakery was for sale. Its rich history and longevity in an

*"We blend ancient, classic techniques with modern thinking, ideas, and local ingredients."*

ever-changing city intrigued me. Orwashers has survived seventeen United States presidents, several economic upturns and downturns, and both World Wars. Its history is unmatchable, and I felt compelled to become a part of it.

When Orwashers Bakery first opened its doors in 1916, it continued the long, rich history of European bakeries that had come before it, serving up old world breads like traditional seeded rye, challah, and pumpernickel to the European immigrants who lived on the Upper East Side of Manhattan. The customers shopped more or less daily, buying freshly baked bread by the pound for their families. I am proud to say that, after taking over the ownership of the almost one-hundred-year-old bakery in 2007, Orwashers still continues this long-standing tradition of serving its Upper East Side neighbors the same hearty, old world breads, freshly baked every day.

Unlike many other artisanal bakeries that work hard to be the freshest, trendiest, or most unique store on the block, at Orwashers our benchmark is not something modern or of the future; it is of the past. We have reached back with flour-covered fingers in order to preserve the traditional breads from one hundred years ago, while at the same time procuring the future of artisanal bread making. In order to do that, we had to ask ourselves a few very important questions: How did our ancestors bake these robust, long-lasting, airy loaves of bread? Furthermore, how do we take what we know of the past and improve it for the customers we are serving today?

Our inspiration is our past. We rely on people, not machines, just as bakers did hundreds of years ago, to control the quality of our bread—creating, tasting, adjusting, and fine-tuning our recipes. Our bakers are passionate craftsmen who willingly engage in our slow, proven ritual. We follow traditional rules of bread-making—hand shaping, cutting, and baking—for breads that give just the right amount of resistance when held and fill the air with a memorable, timeless scent, which says fresh baked right here, right now . . . because they are.

*"For me, baking is a passionate discipline that presents a daily challenge."*

A typical morning at Orwashers Bakery: Keith surrounded by loaves of freshly baked bread.

We pay attention to our preferments—our starters, levains, and bigas, which are alive, growing, and in need of constant care and nurturing. We blend ancient, classic techniques with more modern thinking, ideas, and local ingredients. We believe in long fermentation times to extract complex, delicious flavors, just as bakers did over one hundred years ago. And we always, always, always eat what we bake. Today. One hundred years ago. Forever.

For me, baking is a passionate discipline that presents a daily challenge—a challenge I love: to achieve that magical crust-to-crumb ratio. I didn't wake up one morning and say to myself, "I want to be a bread baker," but I realized early on that I wanted to be the very best at what I do, and baking, it turns out, is what I do. What makes baking such a unique discipline? It calls upon so many different skills and areas of curiosity; it requires creativity, analysis, and troubleshooting. There is a history to the art of bread making, and a science to understanding how flour and water and yeast combine, and under what conditions to create that tasty comforting loaf that can be duplicated again and again. Baking requires the perfect mix of understanding history, chemistry, and physics, and an intense curiosity to discover how things work, all of which has been with me since I was a child. Baking gives me the ability to be incredibly creative, while satisfying my mechanical intuitions and thirst for science; tweaking the recipes has a huge effect on the product, so the kitchen becomes a laboratory. Almost the reverse of cooking, where you kill an animal or pick a vegetable from its roots to make your meal, baking actually requires you to create a living organism with live bacteria and cultures in order to achieve your finished product—an astounding and magical ability. Honestly (aside from the obvious, of course), how many times in life does a person actually get to create a living thing?

My hope in writing this book is to be able to offer anyone who has ever been intoxicated by the smell of baking bread, or has ever torn into a warm, soft loaf fresh out of the oven and thought, "I want to know how to make that," a taste of this intensely passionate discipline—along with the techniques to bake the kind and quality of bread that, for centuries, could only be found behind the closed doors of your corner bakery.

# Chapter 1

# Orwashers Yesterday, Today, and Tomorrow

When Orwashers opened in 1916 on East 78th street in the Yorkville neighborhood of Manhattan, horses still galloped up and down Fifth Avenue instead of taxis, and the source of home entertainment came from the record player in the parlor—not the television. In the almost one hundred years that Orwashers has been serving the people of the Upper East Side, it has been a part of not only creating history, but preserving it. Every day, there is a lineage and heritage poured into the freshly baked breads—a special ingredient, if you will—that invokes the past in order to catapult Orwashers into the future.

New York in 1916 was a very different city than it is today. To set the stage: Woodrow Wilson was president of the United States, World War I was raging abroad but America still remained neutral, and immigrants were storming the doors of Ellis Island by the thousands, seeking refuge in New York City. Between 1860 and 1916, more than twenty-five million immigrants came to the United States, mostly from Europe. By 1910, there was a foreign-born population in New York of approximately two million people. Many of these immigrants settled in tenements on the Lower East

Our shop on East 78th Street today is still the friendly neighborhood bakery.

Side of Manhattan. These were usually three- to five-story apartment buildings that housed many families—sometimes more than twenty! Families lived in a three-room apartment all together, which meant that one apartment could house upwards of ten people. Around the mid-1800s, the Lower East Side became known as Little Germany, due to the large numbers of German immigrants who had settled there during the first wave of immigration that began around 1840. The second wave of immigration, around 1880, brought many other cultures from Central and Eastern Europe, including Polish, Russian, Hungarian, Slovak, Italian, and more German immigrants.

As more and more immigrants poured into Manhattan, many of the Germans who had settled on the Lower East Side began to migrate to the Upper East and West sides. In 1904 the Slocum Disaster occurred. German immigrants from Little Germany had chartered a boat, the General Slocum, for an annual church outing to a picnic site in Eatons Neck, Long Island. Shortly after the trip got underway, a fire started in the lamp room. The ship sank just off the shores of the Bronx and an estimated 1,021 people (many of them women and children) were either burned to death or drowned. The population of Little Germany was greatly decreased and shortly thereafter, it faded away entirely, with the majority of the remaining immigrants moving to the area of Manhattan then known as Yorkville and many of those from other ethnicities soon following suit.

By the early 1900s, the neighbors that Orwashers Bakery served were immigrants from Hungary, Poland, Czechoslovakia, and of course, Germany. At this time, people were still shopping for their groceries and necessities at specialty stores specific to those needs. They bought their meat from the butcher and their bread from the baker, and the milkman delivered their milk. Electricity was still very much a luxury, as was the presence of a refrigerator; most tenement buildings in Yorkville didn't have either. Food didn't stay fresh for long, so people would go shopping every day. Because of this lifestyle, people were much more focused on bread than we are today. The neighborhood baker was an integral part of food shopping. Bread was wholesome, filling, and less expensive than many other foods. People were used to eating it fresh daily.

*"Every day, there is a lineage and heritage poured into the freshly baked breads, a special ingredient that invokes the past."*

The Yorkville neighborhood in the early 1900s was very much like an old European town, and so it followed that Orwashers operated much like an old-fashioned, European bakery that served the town's needs. People wanted to come in and find breads they were used to eating in their old hometown, an ocean—and what may have seemed like a lifetime—away. The typical way to buy bread was from a large communal loaf, usually around eight to ten pounds in weight. The customers would come in and ask for one pound, two pounds, or another amount to feed their families for dinner, and their orders would get cut from the large loaf. Sometimes people would invest in a communal loaf with their neighbors and share it. Orwashers keeps up this tradition by baking one ten-pound, old-fashioned seeded rye bread daily and selling it by the pound as homage to the past, and in an effort to keep this rich, communal tradition alive.

When I first walked into Orwashers in 2007, I was transported back to my grandfather's butcher shop in Kew Gardens, Queens. The clientele he would have served in his neighborhood kosher butcher shop was very much the same as those who originally sought fresh-baked bread at Orwashers. Like a lingering scent, the shop seemed to exude a friendliness and intimacy that comes with the one-on-one interaction of a long line of bakers and shoppers. It felt familiar. It felt like home.

When I took over ownership of the bakery from the Orwasher family, much had changed in the world and neighborhood around the bakery. In the 1950s, 60s, and 70s, the invention of commercial-style loaves and the bread slicer would dilute and alter the process, taste, and experience of eating the breads to which this earlier generation of immigrants was accustomed. Today customers are more familiar with individual loaves. Homes are all equipped with electricity and refrigerators to keep bread cold or even frozen for days. Society's drive to produce everything faster, cheaper, and at a higher volume has caused a shift away from quality; producers have abandoned locally made and natural products and ingredients for less expensive, less pure equivalents such as chemically enhanced, bleached, and bromated flours. Equating the types of foods that

*"Orwashers operated much like an old-fashioned, European bakery that served the town's needs."*

have lined the shelves at grocery stores and overtaken the average person's diet in the last seventy years to those of the past is like comparing a hot dog to a filet mignon. In a span of one hundred years, society's view of bread and what it stands for has changed significantly. What was once thought of as a wholesome staple became known as something that packed on calories—and inches—and offered no nutrients or substance, thanks to its new method of mass production. Traditionally baked artisanal breads are given the time and care they need to ferment and bake to perfection. However, in an effort to give them a longer shelf-life, most mass-produced breads aren't baked for long enough. Therefore, the question facing me as artisanal baker when I purchased Orwashers old-fashioned, European-style bakery soon became: How can I bring back the bread of yesterday while serving the new customer of today, and hopefully tomorrow? The answer? I brought back the old methods of bread baking and preparation while keeping in mind my target consumer. What better place to merge the best of the past with the best of the present than at Orwashers.

At the time of the takeover, Orwashers hadn't changed much about its original ways of operating. It was still baking breads for that Eastern European immigrant of the early 1900s, although the city of New York and the neighborhood of Yorkville had changed significantly. The original recipes from the Orwasher family were oral; directives such as a pinch of this and a dash of that were their only measures of consistency. Though Orwashers still had loyal customers, people weren't buying bread the same way anymore. They didn't want bread by the pound—they wanted loaves and dinner rolls and breads perfect for sandwiches. They wanted newer, more contemporary types of breads. And most importantly, they wanted consistency. They wanted to walk into the bakery and buy a loaf of Italian bread, or sourdough, or cinnamon raisin and have it smell and taste the same way every time. In order for the new Orwashers to be a profitable business, I needed to figure out a way to streamline the process, taste, and experience of the artisanal breads that Orwashers had been making for almost a century. However, the business of Orwashers wasn't the only thing that was almost one hundred years old—the building that housed the bakery was an old tenement building, and the ovens built into the foundation were just as ancient. Some of the breads I was used to making in my previous tenure at the artisanal bread wholesaler, I wasn't able to bake in these ovens. From a business standpoint, it was incredibly important that I increase sales. This meant installing a newer, steam-injected oven, and deciding which breads to keep on our menu and which breads to retire or replace. Little by little I weeded out the offerings, either because I thought particular bread wasn't up to par or because it didn't move enough volume. But some breads were kept out of tradition. Orwashers will always offer traditional rye breads, pumpernickels, and challahs because they are the staples and foundation of the business, but the difference between the Orwashers of yesterday and the Orwashers of today is that I have worked tirelessly to create back-to-basics, scientific, and replicable recipes for the traditional breads, as well as my new creations. The goal was to reinvigorate the bakery by bringing it back to its roots: local flour, old-world techniques, and longer fermentation times. Additionally, I planned to expose the bakery to baking techniques and flavors that would be present in other countries—not just the Eastern European origins of the late nineteenth-century and early twentieth-century immigrants. I vowed to go beyond the past of challahs and ryes and offer more global breads from France, Italy, and Switzerland, amongst others.

In order to create this new method, I became inspired by the past. I pictured myself as a baker in France two hundred years ago, prior to refrigeration, prior to electricity, prior to modern amenities, and asked the most basic question: How did they make this great product? Today we have mechanical mixers, but back then, bakers had to manually knead the bread. There's only so much dough a person can knead by hand without cramping and tiring, leaving the dough still in need of some development. So, what did bakers do hundreds of years ago to add this development to their dough? In lieu of mechanical mixing, they left the dough out to ferment longer. Another crucial difference is that before the mid-nineteenth century, there was no commercial yeast. Bakers had to use old-world dough levains, bigas, and starters. But instead of just returning to these old-world techniques and

We use all natural olives imported from Greece to make our Olive Bread.

ingredients exactly as they were hundreds of years ago, I realized that I needed to change things up ever so slightly in order to be successful in this new-age economy. The levains, bigas, and starters are living organisms that need to be fed and nurtured. Just like the old-world measurements in the original Orwashers recipes that cited a pinch of this and a dash of that, old-world treatment of the starters also wasn't sufficient for ensuring their preservation or consistency. Even the old starters needed a little refreshing. Over time, things get adulterated—people forget to feed the starters on time, or they don't add the right amount of flour or water—we're only human, after all. With this in mind, I decided to refresh and rebuild the starters every year so they would remain extremely robust and incredibly authentic. This also allows the starters to be rid of any potential commercial yeast in the air that may have seeped into them.

I have also expanded the menu significantly to include new, wine- and beer-infused breads and the first 100 percent locally grown ultimate whole-wheat bread, to name just a few. In conjunction with these new modern and worldly breads, I placed a renewed emphasis on sourcing locally whenever possible and always opting for sustainable, natural, and organic ingredients. I strongly believe in the local movement, and feel it is incredibly helpful for local economies. In the last few years, there has been a huge shift back toward local flour farming and milling, which in the past had been pushed farther west by the Erie Canal and developments in technology and transportation. This resurgence of local flour farms and mills not only boosts my local state's economy, but it enhances artisanal baking tremendously. Flour can be a very temperamental ingredient, and is constantly being affected and changed by the soil, climate, and farmer's treatment. While larger mills can compensate for these irregularities in the flour, local mills do not, and opt to leave the grain virtually untouched and unrefined. This is where artisanal baking benefits from local ingredients: our handcrafted breads actually thrive on these variables in local flour. After all, the point of proper artisanal bread is to bring out the fullest, most flavorful taste in the grain. Local ingredients help us do this.

Nearly one hundred years after Orwashers first opened its doors, the bakery is still serving its neighbors. The freshly baked breads can be found on dinner tables, in restaurants, and at farmers' markets all across New York City. One of my focuses is to collaborate with like-minded artisans who share the same values, such as the Channing Daughters Vineyard on Long Island and Sixpoint Brewery in Brooklyn, to craft creative new-world breads with old-world taste. I am also continually looking for new bread experiences to carry Orwashers forward into a future that I am certain will include clients who want new, quality, artisan bread choices.

Bread is perhaps the most universal food that exists. It supersedes prejudices; it appeals to almost every palate; it symbolizes peace, comfort, and tradition. A properly baked loaf of artisanal bread should boast the perfect crackle in its crust and soft crumb that almost disintegrates in your mouth. Something so powerful needs to be nurtured, perfected, loved—and of course, eaten!

At Orwashers, we aren't just bread bakers. We're bread architects.

Vilma, who has been with the bakery 18 years, shows off a freshly baked loaf of Sourdough Bread.

Each day, Orwashers bakes, on average, 4,000 loaves of bread.

# Chapter 2

# ORWASHERS BREAD 101

As with most disciplines, there is a structured process one can follow when learning how to bake bread that is taught in culinary kitchens across the world. Unlike cooking, which lends itself to whimsical experimentation, baking is more like a precise science that requires adherence to specific measurements and correctly executed techniques to achieve successful results. This basic guide—perfect for beginner and novice bread bakers—is broken down into twelve steps, each step aimed at aiding us on our way to procuring the perfect artisanal loaf of bread.

As bread architects, our main goal is to bring forth the most complex, most robust taste from the grains we use and present that taste inside mouthfuls of perfectly baked crusts and crumbs. What does this mean, exactly? Well, baking the perfect loaf isn't just about the taste—it's about the consistency. The crust of the bread is the hard, outer skin of the bread; the crumb is the term used to describe the whole inside of a loaf of bread. Different types of breads call for different consistencies within the crust and crumb. Some breads are dense and some are fluffy, some have a thick crust and some have a flakier crust, some are sour and some are sweet. Bakers in the know can cut open a loaf of freshly baked bread and tell you all about the bread's hydration levels, the types of flour that were used, how much or how little yeast was used, as well as how the dough was shaped and mixed, simply by looking closely at the crust and crumb. Despite their differences, all artisan breads require proper fermentation, careful use of steam and heat, accurate measuring, and high-quality ingredients. In general, the longer dough ferments, the tastier it will be. However, this does depend on what kind of bread you are baking. As a rule, lean breads, meaning breads that use minimal basic ingredients (flour, water, yeast) such as the French baguette, benefit from long fermentation times because they get their sweetness and flavor from natural sugars in the grain as opposed to added fat from ingredients like eggs or milk. In breads with added fats, or enriched breads, like brioches, the added sugars make it easier for the dough to overproof, which can leave your bread tasting yeasty. Still, proper fermentation for enriched breads is key for creating the moist, buttery crumb and full flavor. But no matter what type of bread you are baking, these twelve steps will be invaluable on your journey to making bakery-worthy artisanal bread in your very own home.

## Baking Tip:

Baking, just like learning proper baking techniques, takes time. You can't rush fermentation: artificially increasing your dough's temperature by placing on a radiator or warm stovetop will not yield a good loaf of bread.

# HOW DO CRUSTS AND CRUMBS DIFFER IN VARIOUS BREADS?

Here are a variety of traditional breads that you'll learn to make from this book and the distinguishing characteristics of their crusts and crumbs.

**BAGUETTE**

The baguette is a traditional long, narrow French bread. Its crust is generally on the thinner side, and is golden brown and flaky. The crumb has large irregular holes, and is light and airy.

## PULLMANS
Pullman bread has a typically soft crust and crumb, and the crumb is also particularly tight, meaning it is without larger, irregular holes. The Pullman loaf is mostly used for sandwiches, and is the most commercialized. It's baked in a Pullman pan to give it its signature shape.

## PUMPERNICKEL & RYE

Pumpernickel and rye breads generally have tighter crumbs than other breads because the rye berry has less gluten in it, but it is still nice and chewy. The crust is on the thinner side, but traditionally crunchy.

## CIABATTA

Ciabatta is an Italian bread known as a rustic bread for its wetter dough. This bread has a very crispy, thin crust, and an extremely moist, spongy crumb due to its high water content.

## FOCACCIA

Focaccia is made from an extremely soft, wet dough. There are many variations of focaccia, so the crumb can vary from cake-like to moist and spongy depending on the recipe, but is always relatively thick. The crust is thin and crispy.

## CHALLAH

Challah is made from a soft, rich dough enriched with ingredients like eggs. This makes the crumb very moist and soft, while the crust is thin, flaky, and usually glazed.

*Challah is a good example of an enriched bread— one with added fats like egg yolks, while Sourdough is a lean bread—made primarily of flour, water, and yeast.*

## SOURDOUGH

Sourdough bread is always made
from a starter. Its crust is thin
yet crispy, and its crumb is moist
and spongy, with medium-sized
irregular holes.

# STEP 1: GETTING STARTED

The absolute first step to baking bread is to make sure that you have all of the tools and ingredients you will need during this process. *Mise en place* is a French saying, meaning "putting everything in its place." This should ideally happen before you begin baking. While I know this may seem like an arduous task, believe me when I say it is well worth the effort. Make sure to carefully read through the recipe before beginning to bake. Every type of bread is prepared differently, and has its own specific rules and requirements to achieve the perfect flavor, shape, and feel. The last thing you want is to realize you don't have all the needed ingredients, or that the clock on your oven isn't working and you have no idea when the bread went in or how much longer it needs to bake! That said, I've put together a list of major tools that I deem necessary, and minor tools that will come in handy but may be not be required, or may have suitable alternatives.

Whether you have been baking for years, or you have never baked a day in your life, the various tools and equipment that are essential for baking Orwashers recipes may come as a surprise. The recipes in this book have all been crafted with care, precision, and method; and like an experiment in a science lab, the correct equipment must be used to ensure the best and most consistent results.

Assemble all the ingredients and equipment you need for a recipe before you start.

# MAJOR TOOLS

### DIGITAL SCALE

Unlike many other recipes and many other cookbooks, the ingredients listed in my Orwashers recipes are measured strictly by weight, making the use of a digital scale a necessity. While most recipes use cups, teaspoons, and tablespoon measurements, these can still be too inconsistent when it comes to the science of bread making. Not all measuring cups are created equal. Also how compacted ingredients are in the measuring cups can affect the total amounts used. Even a cup of water measured by one person might not be the same as a cup of water measured by someone else; this is the factor of human error. The amount of flour or water needed for any given recipe is so exact that it may not fall within the normal range of measurements by cup or tablespoon, and rounding up or down in this case won't yield a successful outcome. Additionally, different brands and types of a given ingredient will most likely have different weights and physical forms, which can affect your ability to measure them property using measuring tools instead of a scale. For example, all flours aren't created equal; rye flour, whole-wheat flour, and all-purpose white flour do not bear the same weights. Therefore, four cups of whole-wheat flour will have a different weight than four cups of all-purpose flour. But there is little room for fluctuation when using a scale. If the recipe calls for the flour to be measured by weight, you are sure to always have the correct measurement no matter what type of flour you are using. In a recipe that calls for salt or sugar, if the granules you are measuring by volume are larger or smaller than the ones the person who originated the recipe used, your measurement will be off in one direction or the other. But if you weigh the salt and sugar out, it won't matter how big or small the grains are. Without the use of a digital scale for measuring, you will most likely experience some inaccuracies in your finished product.

The scale must measure weight in grams and ounces and account for two spaces after the decimal point. For example, it must be able to measure out 2.23 lbs/1 kg bread flour or .86 lb/390.1 g white flour. Precision is the key to making delicious and consistent bread.

A stand mixer with a fairly high power level will make mixing bread dough much less laborious and give a consistent texture.

## STAND MIXER WITH A DOUGH HOOK

A stand mixer with a dough hook is a vital tool for all of these recipes, and it is the only machine the bakers at Orwashers use. This tool will help with precision with any size batch of dough, but will be particularly helpful when making larger batches. Of course, one can mix with a giant bowl and spoon, but in today's day and age, a stand mixer is an affordable addition to any baker's kitchen, making the process of mixing much less laborious and more manageable for the day-to-day baking.

If you are purchasing a stand mixer, here are some helpful tips. The higher power the mixer, the longer it will last you. Many affordable mixers are around 325 watts of power, which is on the lower end of the power spectrum. Dough can be thick, so getting a mixer with more power—either 500 or 700 watts, or even higher depending on how often you intend to use it—will put less of a strain on the mixer's motor. Make sure the mixer has low, medium, and high settings. Most stand mixers have at least five different speeds, with newer models having nine or ten. The more speeds, the better; different recipes call for different mixing techniques, and dough thicknesses and consistencies vary, so a wider variety is always favorable. It's essential that whatever mixer you buy comes with a dough hook attachment. This is ideal for kneading the dough. The mixer may also come with a paddle attachment that will be useful when mixing denser dough, where the crumb will have smaller, more uniform air holes. The dough hook, however, will be used for nearly every bread recipe. It will fold and stretch the dough uniformly so the gluten strands will develop, which as we will see later is very important to the fermentation process.

## OVEN

It is imperative to use an oven with precise temperature readings. Many of the recipes call for extremely specific temperatures, for example 490°F /255°C. Almost every oven has hot spots, and it can take time to learn where they are and how to navigate them. An oven thermometer, preferably digital, will definitely be an asset for your oven. No matter how precise you think your oven is, you will most likely be surprised to discover how inaccurate the gauge can be. Furthermore, you will be amazed at how much better everything you make in your oven tastes when the temperature is controlled and accurate. Remember that baking is a process, and part of that process is getting to know your oven and how the dough reacts to it. It may take many tweaks before reaching the perfect outcome.

Discovering your oven's hot spots and quirks can be time consuming but the reward is consistently baked, delicious bread.

# MINOR TOOLS

### MIXING BOWL

For mixing, resting, and proofing dough, some large mixing bowls will come in handy. These can be any material: glass, plastic, wooden, stainless steel, etc. Just make sure whatever you use is big enough for your batch of dough. You should leave enough room for the dough to double in volume as it rises.

### DOUGH SCRAPER

This tool will make portioning and transporting the dough easier. Use the dull edge so it will not ruin your work surface.

### OVEN THERMOMETER

Most ovens—even very expensive ones—can become less accurate over time. Also, most ovens have hot and cold spots to navigate. An oven thermometer will help with accuracy. The best kind of oven thermometer is a digital probe thermometer that allows you to read the temperature gauge without opening the oven and thus altering the temperature you are trying to read.

Mixing bowls need to be big enough to allow the dough to double in size when it's time for rising.

## WOODEN CUTTING BOARD

Wooden boards are best for working with dough because they absorb the flour a little bit more than other surfaces. Marble and granite are also good alternatives because the dough sticks less on them than it does on plastic surfaces. The less the dough sticks, the less flour you will need to add during kneading and shaping, which ultimately affects the texture of your bread. Marble and granite surfaces are also likely to absorb less bacteria since they are nonporous. Wood, although porous, does have natural anti-bacterial properties.

## SPRAY BOTTLES

These will come in handy when oiling your pans and baking sheets. You can also put water in them and use them to create steam in the oven during baking.

## INSTANT-READ DIGITAL COOKING THERMOMETER

A standard, digital cooking thermometer is important for taking the temperature of the water used in the recipe, as well as the dough throughout the mixing process.

## BAKING STONE
## (OFTEN REFERRED TO AS A PIZZA STONE)

A baking stone may be necessary to get the oven to reach the highest temperatures that are required of some of these recipes. You can also opt to use one of these to improve your oven's accuracy, even if your oven can reach the highest temperatures. The baking stone will absorb the heat in the oven and radiate it all over consistently, similar to how a brick oven works. It helps even out the hot spots in the oven and offers the dough a more even baking experience overall, allowing for the ideal crust and crumb outcome.

## OTHER USEFUL TOOLS:

Loaf pans in various sizes
Baking sheets
Pastry wheel cutter or pizza wheel
Parchment paper
Mixing spoons
Peels

BAKING FACT:

The baking stone may be one of the oldest pieces of "kitchen equipment." It was used as long ago as 45,000 BC to bake a flat bread over an open fire pit, that was a staple of Stone Age man. Then as now, the stone absorbs moisture and produces a crisp crust on the bread.

# BAKER'S MATH

Bread baking may not seem like a science, but in order to create a rustic ciabatta that is light and aromatic or to yield a Chardonnay miche that boasts a dark-baked crust and a tangy, chewy interior, one must treat the ingredients with the care and exactitude that a science requires.

While most bread recipes—including the ones in this book—are presented in measurement form, professional bakers tend to use *bread formulas* instead of exact recipes. In the science of bread baking, each and every ingredient must be measured *in ratio* to the other ingredients in order to produce the optimal outcome. A recipe includes measured ingredients for a very specific batch of bread. However, adjustments are almost always necessary due to a variety of factors, including storage and room temperature, heat and humidity of the day, tools, and the quality of ingredients, for example. If you find yourself having to adjust a recipe mid-process, you can do this easily by knowing the percentage that each ingredient is in ratio to the others. The process of baking bread is all about controlling your outcome, and ensuring it is exactly how you intended it to be. Being able to adjust your recipe to counteract unforeseen problems or to allow you to be more creative is something every baker should aspire to. This precise technique of converting recipes into percentages is commonly referred to as Baker's Math, and these are the basics that every baker should adopt in his or her laboratory.

The Baker's Math formula is the ratio of ingredients in a recipe. Understanding this method allows for easier communication between bakers, and easier and more accurate conversions of recipes to varying size batches. In this formula, all ingredients in a given recipe are measured in relation to the amount/percentage of flour in that recipe. Experienced bakers will learn average percentages for certain ingredients over time. For example, most experienced bakers know that the percentage of water or hydration in most lean breads falls within 55 percent to 65 percent of the flour weight, and higher for enriched breads like Focaccia. Salt usually falls within 1.5 percent to 2.5 percent of the flour weight.

To convert a recipe into a Baker's Math formula, you always start with the flour. The flour in any given recipe will always equal 100 percent. If you are using a recipe that calls for more than one type of flour, the combination of the flours will equal 100 percent. **You should also be aware that the percentages of each ingredient in a recipe shouldn't add up to 100 percent, so don't allow this to confuse you.** Every other ingredient gets converted into a percentage based on the amount of flour by doing basic math conversions.

# BAKER'S MATH FORMULA FOR ORWASHERS CABERNET RUSTICA

Recipe measurements in grams

Bread Flour: 1,000

Water: 671.30

Levain: 467.20 (White Flour: 224.26; Water: 242.94)

Salt: 36.30

Instant Yeast: 9.10

Since you know that the flour must equal 100%, you will always start your conversion with the flour. You also know that you must include all different types of flours in this percentage.

1,000 (bread flour) + 224.26 (white flour in levain) = 1,224.26

Therefore 1,224.26=100%

You can calculate the percentages of the remaining ingredients by multiplying the number of grams of each ingredient by 100, then dividing it by the number of grams in the flour. So, for example:

671.30 + 242.94 grams of water equals 914.24 grams of water. Multiply that by 100 = 91,424. 91,424 divided by 1,224.26 equals 74.68%.

Similarly,

$$\frac{36,300 \text{ grams of salt}}{1,224.26 \text{ grams of flour}} = 2.97\% \qquad \frac{9,100 \text{ grams of yeast}}{1,224.26 \text{ grams of flour}} = .74\%$$

Working the remaining ingredients through this formula, this is the original recipe converted to Baker's Math percentages:

Bread Flour & White Flour: 100%

Water: 74.68%

Salt: 2.97%

Instant Yeast: .74%

---

Total: 178.39%

# STEP 2: MIXING TECHNIQUES

There are many different techniques one can use to mix dough, but the purpose of this step is always the same: to evenly distribute the ingredients so your dough is uniform, to allow the gluten to develop, and to begin the initial fermentation.

The first step is always to combine and incorporate the flour, water, yeast, preferment, and salt together in a mixing bowl. When doing this, be cognizant of the fact that if the salt comes in direct contact with the yeast, the salt will kill it. That's why, in the recipes in this book the yeast is often added after the salt has been incorporated with other ingredients or, if the salt and yeast are added at the same time, it's in conjunction with other ingredients to form a buffer between the salt and the yeast.

The next step is to mix the dough to develop the gluten. As a general rule, the longer dough is mixed, the tighter the crumb structure will become. Alternatively, the less the dough is mixed, the more airy it becomes, allowing for an open and irregular cell structure. Some bakers choose to knead by hand, while others mix their dough with a stand mixer. Kneading the dough by hand means to work the dough in a continuous motion by folding, stretching, and pressing until it is uniform. The stand mixer with the dough hook attachment mimics this kneading process mechanically. Some bakers do a combination of both hand mixing and electric mixing techniques. There are positives and negatives to each technique. Hand mixing or kneading allows one to get a feel for the dough and often ensures that the dough will never get overmixed. Mixing with a stand mixer is easier, especially when baking a large batch. At Orwashers, we always mix with a stand mixer because of the large quantities we are producing on a daily basis.

As you make more bread you'll begin to be able to "feel" when your dough is mixed enough.

# TO KNEAD BY HAND OR TO USE A STAND MIXER? THAT IS THE QUESTION …

If you're new to bread baking, you might be wondering what the specific benefits and drawbacks are to each option. Here are a few:

## HAND MIXING:

1. It is harder to overheat the dough this way, since you don't have the added friction of the electric mixer.

2. You learn to feel the gluten strands develop, which is a very helpful skill.

3. With this method, you will rarely overmix your dough.

4. There's a certain romance and artisanship to kneading your dough by hand that some people don't want to give up.

5. Kneading by hand regularly can cause strain to your hands and wrists over time.

6. You also run the risk of undermixing and underdeveloping the gluten strands.

## STAND MIXING:

1. The stand mixer does a great job mixing and kneading the dough evenly.

2. Depending on how fast you knead by hand, the stand mixer can potentially do the job much faster.

3. This technique is better for larger batches of dough.

4. Stand mixers tend to travel across the counter, so be aware of this and keep an eye on your mixer.

5. The friction from the stand mixer will add a couple degrees to the temperature of your dough, so this is something to keep in mind in terms of the final internal dough temperature.

## IF THE WATER IS MEASURED EXACTLY, HOW CAN THE DOUGH *STILL* OVERHYDRATE?

It is important to note that every bag of flour is different in terms of its water absorption, even if it is the same type of flour or the same brand. Not every yield of grain coming from the farm is exactly the same; there are many agricultural factors that influence the final product. Recipes may need to be adjusted by 1 or 2 percent in either direction (more or less water) depending on how the flour is absorbing the water.

Evenly distributing all of the ingredients while mixing is essential for creating a consistent product. If you are using a preferment, a live yeast culture, make sure to distribute this evenly throughout the dough as well so the whole loaf can benefit from its advantages. Always begin mixing with all of the flour inside the mixing bowl. Next, add about 75 percent of the recipe's suggested water measurement, and begin to mix. Once all of that water has been incorporated, slowly add the last 25 percent of the water. Make sure not to overhydrate the dough as you mix. Overhydrated dough is very sticky, to the point where it will be difficult to get it out of the mixing bowl. Some particularly hard grains, like gluten-free grains or whole-wheat grains, could benefit from presoaking. This allows them time to absorb the hydration better, softening their harsh starches, which makes them easier to digest. If you presoak grains in your recipe, I would recommend taking all the water from your recipe and soaking your grains in that. Then add the grain, along with any water not absorbed during soaking, to the flour in the mixing bowl. Be aware that you may need to add additional water when mixing. Once the flour has incorporated the water, you can add the salt, yeast, and preferment as instructed above.

In order to develop the gluten properly, a kneading rhythm should be adopted to work the dough continuously—especially if you are mixing the dough by hand. Since one of the main purposes of mixing is to develop the gluten, you need to be careful not to tear the gluten strands that you are actually creating during mixing.

What is gluten and how does it develop? Gluten is the main protein in wheat. It consists of two parts—glutenin and gliadin—that combine when they are hydrated to form gluten, and are responsible for adding structure and flavor to the bread. Brands and types of flours have varying gluten contents, and therefore some may require more or less time to develop than others during this stage. Whether the dough is being mixed and kneaded by hand, or with a stand mixer, it should look shiny and smooth, and feel springy to the touch, bouncing back when it is gently poked. The best way to determine whether you have developed the gluten enough during mixing is called the Windowpane Test.

Every type of flour is different and absorbs varying amounts of water based on how much protein is in its grains. Therefore, every type of flour reacts differently to the amount of hydration added. This is why recipes are never 100 percent accurate; as a baker, you should be prepared to adjust any given recipe accordingly to control your desired outcome. If you have added all the hydration the recipe suggested, and you feel that your dough is still too stiff, this may be due to conditions outside of your control that were not accounted for in the recipe. In this case, you should add more water, little by little, until you arrive at your desired dough consistency.

Once the hydration is added to your ingredients, not only is the gluten formed, but the yeast will absorb the water during the mixing process and begin to leaven. This is the initial fermentation. If you are using commercial active dry yeast, this will need to be hydrated first before being added to the ingredients. Both preferments and active yeast will absorb enough hydration during mixing to begin fermentation.

## THE WINDOWPANE DOUGH TEST:

Perform this test to see if the dough has been mixed or kneaded enough.

1. Cut off a small amount of dough, roughly the size of an egg.

2. Hold it between your thumb and first two fingers with both hands.

3. Spread your fingers and thumbs apart, stretching the dough.

4. You should be able to see translucency in the middle part of the dough, similar to a windowpane.

5. If the dough is not translucent, mix for an additional two minutes and try again.

## HOW DO ADDITIONAL INGREDIENTS AFFECT THE DOUGH?

You should always add additional ingredients like olives, nuts, or dried fruits at the very end of mixing, stopping as soon as the ingredients have been incorporated throughout the dough. This will ensure you do not overmix the dough, as well as protect the ingredients from becoming damaged during mixing. When you add these types of ingredients, you will have to increase the yeast or water content or both, depending on what type of flavor you want to achieve. If you are weighing down the dough with heavy ingredients like nuts or olives, you will need more yeast to get the bread to rise. See Chapter 7 for more on experimentation with additional ingredients.

## SALT

Earlier on in this section, I mentioned that it is vital to keep the salt and the yeast separate during the initial mixing of the ingredients or else the salt will kill off the yeast. Salt plays several roles in the bread-making process, and is an extremely important ingredient. Because of this, using the correct amount of salt in your bread is crucial. Too much salt, and your bread won't be edible. Too little, and your bread will rise too quickly, lack color, and taste bland.

The first thing to understand about salt is that its presence slows down yeast fermentation. Salt naturally absorbs moisture. As we know, during the initial fermentation the yeast cells absorb the water and begin to leaven. The salt will want to pull that moisture away from the yeast and absorb it, so if the yeast and salt come in direct contact with one another, the yeast will lack the moisture it needs to work and will eventually die. Keeping the yeast and salt separate during the initial mixing is vital to keep the yeast alive, and still allows the salt to affect the fermentation process even after it is completely mixed in, which is necessary for full flavor development. Too much or too little salt will affect your final outcome in several ways. If you have too much salt, it will slow down the fermentation too much and reduce the volume of the dough. However, if there is not enough salt, the dough will ferment too quickly to develop those rich, robust flavors we are striving to achieve. While this may seem like a daunting balancing act, achieving the correct amount of salt is critical in controlling the dough's fermentation and ultimately the final product.

Salt affects the taste, texture, and appearance of bread.

## FINAL DOUGH TEMPERATURE

After you are done mixing the dough for the allotted time (e.g. two minutes on low, followed by five minutes on high), you will need to take the temperature of your dough. Do this using an instant-read digital cooking thermometer. For fermenting, rising, and proofing to happen at the appropriate rate, the ideal temperature for the dough is somewhere between 72°F and 76°F (22°C and 24°C). Taking the temperature at different points throughout the mixing process will also help you avoid undermixing and overmixing as the friction of mixing causes dough temperature to rise.

There are a variety of elements that can, and do, affect the temperature of the dough. These include the temperature in the air, the type of flour, the amount of friction created during mixing, and the temperature of the preferment used. The temperature of the room the bread is fermenting in is extremely important—dough fermenting in a 65°F (18°C) room will need double the time of dough fermenting in a 75°F (24°C) room. That said, pumping your room temperature up to 75°F (24°C) might seem like a good shortcut, but remember: Without proper fermentation time, your bread will lack the complex flavors you are hoping to achieve. In general, slower fermentation is always better.

It is perfectly fine to use tap water for your hydration, provided it's not abnormally high in chlorine or minerals. Whatever kind of water you use, it is important to play around with the temperature of the water. You can use your thermometer for this as well. If you mix the dough with water that is too cold, your final dough temperature will be lower; this in turn will result in dough that will take much longer to rise, and you run the risk of the dough getting old as you wait for it to rise. If you mix the dough with water that is too hot, your dough will run away on you—rising and fermenting much too quickly. Without the proper fermentation time, the dough won't develop the complex flavors that should be present in the final product. When using a stand mixer, the ideal temperature for added water should fall somewhere between 50°F and 55°F (10°C and 13°C). When mixing by hand, the water temperature can be a touch higher.

## HOW DOES A STAND MIXER AFFECT THE TEMPERATURE OF THE DOUGH?

It is important to keep in mind that every mixer is different. The friction from your mixer will increase the temperature of your dough, simply by doing its job. Mixing with a stand mixer involves much more friction than mixing or kneading by hand. This friction will add a couple of degrees to your dough temperature. Low and high speeds vary from mixer to mixer. The higher the speed, the more friction. You need to be able to think critically about how your mixer is getting the job done and be able to adjust the process accordingly.

Oxygenation is the process by which air gets incorporated into the dough. Too much oxygen will compromise the compounds formed by the gluten molecules and destroy the carotenoids in the flour that help give it its color and taste. Therefore, too much oxidation leads to a washed-out color in the crust as well as dulled flavor in the crumb.

# STEP 3: FERMENTATION

If I had to choose the most important stage of the baking process, this would be it. My whole philosophy when I bought and relaunched Orwashers was to bring us back to the past with method baking—to go back to old-world traditions—and this is the stage where that philosophy pays off. This is where the rich preferments and starters really do their work, fermenting for long periods of time, enriching the dough with every passing minute. This is when the dough gains all of its flavor. If fermentation is not carried out properly, your final product will reveal this. You cannot make up for this mistake in other stages of the process, so it is vital that you are focused and attentive during this stage. The dough fermentation is what allows a once dense ball of dough to transform into the flavorful, risen loaf of bread.

As the dough temperature plays an important role in this part of the process, it is still important to keep a close watch on this while the dough ferments. This can be tricky at home since, unlike a bakery, your kitchen is most likely not a controlled environment. Keep in mind that outside temperatures can greatly affect the temperature of your room, as well. If you are baking in the wintertime, you might have become accustomed to the coldness of your kitchen—but the dough won't be! Be mindful of the clock; set a timer if necessary to help you keep track of how long the dough has been fermenting and how much longer you will need to let it sit.

What actually happens during fermentation? During yeast fermentation, the yeast cells in the dough feed off of the sugars in the grain, breaking the molecules apart and allowing them to become accessible. As the yeast breaks these complex carbohydrates into simple sugars, it releases carbon dioxide and ethyl alcohol into the dough, creating bubbles. These sugars go on to caramelize during baking to create those golden brown crusts that are a signature characteristic of all artisanal breads. This is why it is important to only use the exact amount of yeast that you need—not more, not less. Too much yeast will leave the cells without enough sugar to feed on, resulting in an overly alcoholic taste. Too little yeast, and the dough won't rise enough or ferment properly and the taste will be off. If the dough has been properly fermented, there will be enough sugar molecules released to offer the perfect flavor and color during caramelization in the oven and the right amount of starch intact to account for the texture of the crust and crumb.

Once your dough is ready to ferment, place it in a well-greased bowl that is at least twice the size of your dough. Remember, when fully risen the dough will be double its original size, so you need to make sure it won't spill over your bowl. Next, cover your bowl with plastic wrap and let it sit. The amount of fermentation time differs based on the type of bread you are making, as well as many of the other factors previously mentioned—temperature, brand of flour, environment, and so on. Fermentation can take anywhere from an hour to overnight, depending on the recipe and desired outcome.

Beneath the surface of this seemingly quietly rising dough, yeast is breaking complex carbohydrates into simple sugars, which releases carbon dioxide and creates bubbles.

# STEP 4: PUNCHING DOWN OR DEGASSING

The next step in the process is known as punching down or degassing. There are several reasons for this step. First, as mentioned above, during fermentation, the yeast releases carbon dioxide and alcohol, creating bubbles in the dough. Therefore, bakers must apply pressure to the dough to get rid of some of this excess carbon dioxide. If too much carbon dioxide is left, it will halt the yeast fermentation and create large holes in your crumb. Second, punching the dough continues to help with the gluten development, allowing it to take a break. There are a lot of chemicals in the dough that, without given time to rest from fermentation, would begin to break down the gluten strands that have thus far formed. Third, the temperature of the dough has altered since it was last tested. It is most likely much cooler on the outside of the dough than it is at the center, so this process helps even that out. And finally, it redistributes the yeast, so it ferments evenly across the dough and will rise evenly when the dough is baked.

Different breads require different amounts of degassing. It all depends on your desired outcome. Some bread requires more gas to create larger, irregular holes in the crumb, like airy baguettes and ciabattas; in this case, only a small amount of degassing is necessary. For breads with medium-sized holes, like dinner or sandwich rolls, you should degas a bit more than very airy loaves but not as long as a denser loaf. If you are looking to create a really dense crumb, you should degas for a longer period of time. While the step calls for "punching down," it is important to be gentle with your dough when degassing so as not to destroy the gluten strands you have formed. You want a strong blow to knock out some of the bubbles but you do not want to squeeze the dough and eliminate all air bubbles.

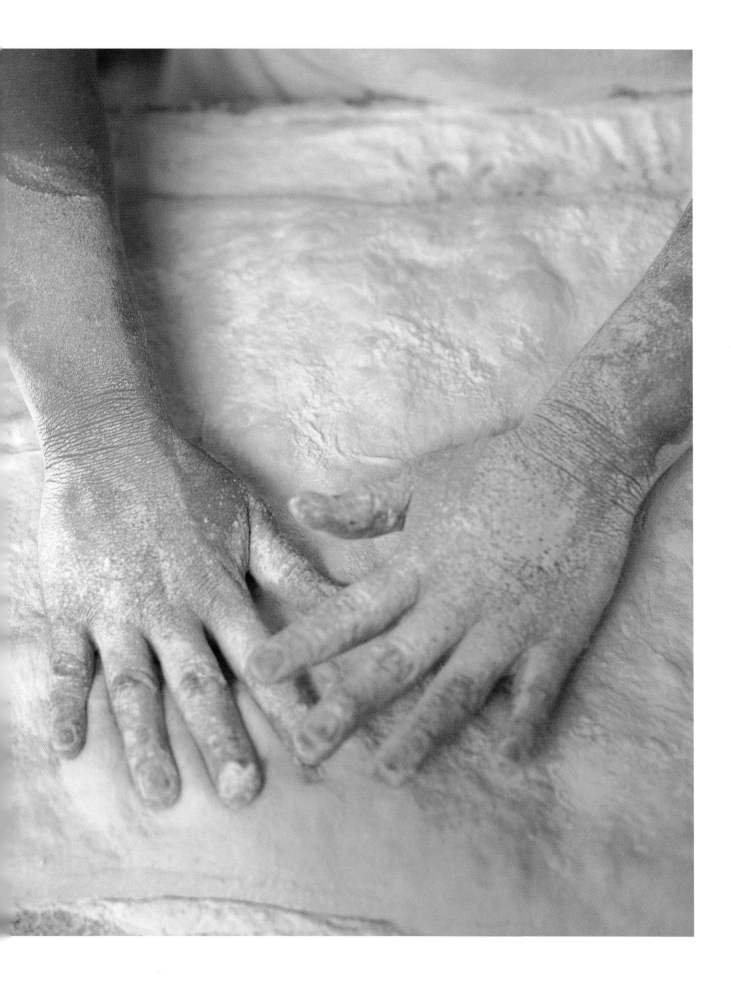

# STEP 5: DIVIDING

Once the dough has been degassed, it is ready to be divided and weighed. Most bread recipes call for two fermentation cycles. The first is done with the bulk dough; the second is performed after the dough has been divided into individual loaves or servings. If you are only making one loaf, you can skip over this step and move right onto Resting, Step 7.

When dividing your dough, cut your pieces cleanly with a sharp, clean knife (not serrated), as opposed to tearing them. Cut the dough in one, smooth motion, without going back and forth. All of this is to avoid tearing the network of gluten strands that has formed during fermentation. Once you have cut the dough into pieces, weigh them to make sure they are the proper size. If you have a piece that is too big, simply cut it the same way you originally cut the dough and gently attach it to the smaller piece. Don't fold or knead these two pieces together; they will connect on their own during the next stages.

# STEP 6: ROUNDING

If you needed to divide your dough into separate loaves, you will need to round your bread before shaping. Once the dough pieces have been divided and weighed, you will round them into their basic intended shape now (which is not necessarily a round shape). Rounding the dough now, prior to the next resting, will make shaping it later on easier. It will strengthen the dough by stretching the gluten and forming the outer skin of your loaf. Since this is just the precursor to shaping, the dough doesn't need too much handling. Once you have shaped it into a rounded form, move onto the next step.

# STEP 7: RESTING (OR BENCHING)

Traditionally, resting is the term used to describe leaving the dough out to rise after mixing but *before* shaping. The purpose of this rest is to, once again, relax the gluten after it has been rounded, and to allow the dough to finish rising. It is important to relax the gluten during resting so that the strands will be more extensible, or able to stretch more easily, during shaping.

In order for dough to rest properly, I suggest that you place the pieces in a well-oiled container and seal it shut. Make sure the container is at least twice the size of your dough. If you don't have any containers, you can place the rounded pieces on a lightly floured surface and cover them with plastic wrap.

While at rest, the gluten strands relax, preparing the dough for shaping.

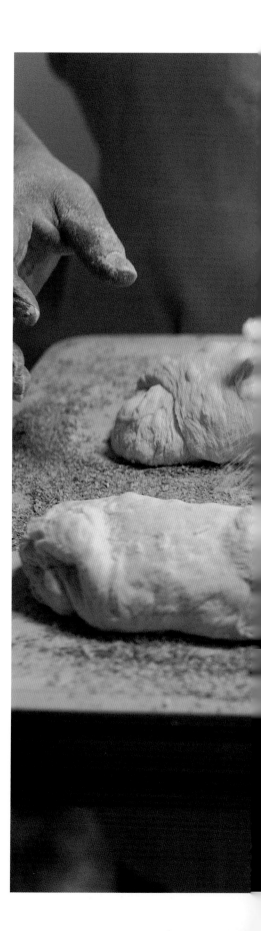

## HOW DO YOU KNOW IF THE DOUGH IS READY TO BE SHAPED?

There are some basic characteristics that can help you determine whether or not your dough has rested enough and is ready for shaping. First is the dough's elasticity, which is defined as its stretchiness, or tendency to snap back to shape after it is stretched. Next is its extensibility, which is its ability to expand and be shaped. The dough must achieve a give and take between these two states before it can be shaped. When the dough is finished resting, it should feel springy and elastic, but with proper techniques you should be able to mold and shape it into your desired shape. If the dough tears when you stretch it, it needs more time to develop the right elasticity and extensibility for shaping.

# STEP 8: SHAPING

Breads come in all shapes and sizes. Some breads are long, like baguettes, while others are rounded, like sourdough. Shape is somewhat of a preference, as different kinds of breads can embody a variety of shapes.

Certain doughs do not lend themselves to being rounded. For instance, breads that are made from very wet doughs, like focaccias, are much harder to shape into a round form because these spongier doughs are more elastic, and therefore less extensible and able to hold the round shape. Wetter dough is more difficult to work with, but when it is made correctly, the finished product will have an aerated crumb and delicious crust. The primary goals of shaping are both aesthetic and structural in nature. You want to bake a loaf that is pleasing to the eye, while ensuring that the crust and crumb bake properly.

If you are baking in a pan, make sure you choose the pan that is the appropriate size for your size dough. If your pan is too small, the dough will bleed over the sides of the pan while baking. If the pan is too large, it might be difficult to gauge whether or not your loaf has risen the proper amount, which can lead to overbaking. Free-form shapes can be baked on baking sheets or baking stones.

What follows are some of the shaping techniques you'll need to make the recipes in Chapters 5 and 6.

## FOLDING TECHNIQUE
1.  Place dough on a lightly floured work surface.
2.  With both hands, grab the bottom left and right corners and pull the bottom ⅓ of the dough up toward the middle.
3.  Following the same technique, fold the top ⅓ of the dough toward the middle.
4.  Following the same technique, fold the left ⅓ of the dough toward the middle.
5.  Following the same technique, fold the right ⅓ of the dough toward the middle.
6.  Then flip the dough over, fold side down. It should look relatively round and smooth.

## WHERE DID THE PULLMAN LOAF GET ITS NAME?

Many people aren't aware that the name for the Pullman loaf shape actually came from the railroad company the Pullman Palace Car Company, which manufactured railway cars in the mid- to late-nineteenth century. Because the kitchens on trains were so compact, the Pullman Company is credited with creating these lidded, square-shaped pans for baking bread on the train—hence the name for any square-shaped, sandwich-style loaf of bread.

## BOULE

The term boule is French for "ball." As you may have guessed, a boule is the traditional shape for French bread—aside from the long, narrow baguette, of course. When shaping a boule, the goal is to give the dough enough surface tension so that the shape will keep through the baking process rather than flatten out.

1.  Take an individual piece of dough and place it on a lightly floured work surface.

2.  Starting at the top, pinch and pull a piece of the dough from the outside into the middle. Continue this method all the way around the outside of the dough, about five or six times. It helps to think of this process as gathering all the points of a star into the middle. Remember: the goal is to create a surface area with enough tension that it will keep its shape during baking.

3.  With the gathering point on the bottom, roll the dough between both hands to make it a solid spherical shape.

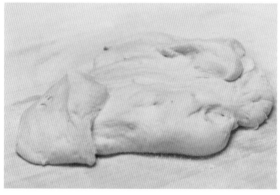

Step 1

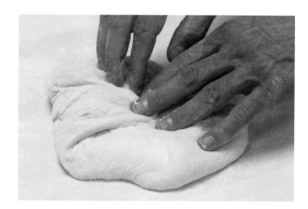

Step 2

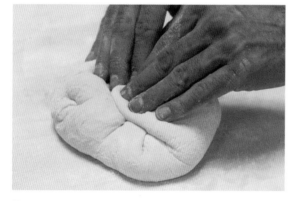

Step 3

The shaped boule

## FREE-FORM OVAL

This rustic shape will give you some consistency in the shape and size of each slice without having to use a Pullman pan. It is particularly good for doughs that are not too wet. This shape is great for most types of levains, rustic breads, and ryes.

1. Take an individual piece of dough and place it on a lightly floured work surface.
2. Fold the left side of the dough about 2 in/5 cm toward the middle.
3. Fold the right side of the dough about 2 in/5 cm toward the middle.
4. Fold both the top and bottom of the dough toward the middle, leaving about an inch of space between them.
5. Starting at the top, fold the dough into itself about one-third of the way down. Repeat this folding method while rolling the dough into a cylindrical shape; make sure to keep tension in the dough's surface area.
6. Roll dough a few times on work surface to make sure the seam is sealed.

Step 1

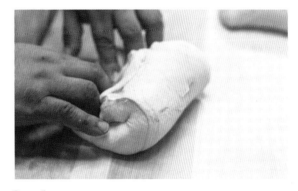

Step 5

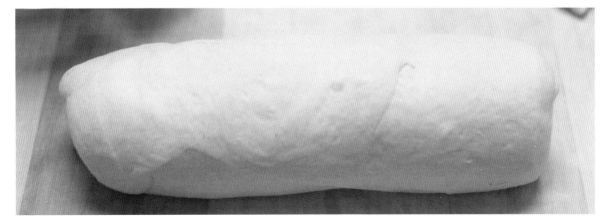

The shaped free-form oval

## FOCACCIA

Focaccia is an Italian bread that is made from a wetter dough; and when baked, the crumb is soft, spongy, and shiny. Focaccia can be either savory or sweet, allowing for many different types of ingredients and flavors. These breads are baked on sheet pans to give them their traditional flat, rectangular shape.

1. Using all of your fingers push dough down repeatedly so that the dough spreads to the edges of the pan.
2. Spray the top of the dough with olive oil.

Step 1

Step 2

## CIABATTA

The ciabatta is another Italian bread, also made from a wetter dough, similar to the focaccia. These doughs are traditionally sticky and difficult to shape, and may need some additional flour to keep it from sticking. Again, like the focaccia, the ciabatta crumb is open, spongy, and shiny.

1. Take the complete batch of dough and place it on a floured work surface.
2. Using all of your fingers, push the dough down repeatedly so that it spreads.
3. Continue this process until the dough is approximately 1 in/2.5 cm thick.
4. Using a pizza cutter, pastry wheel cutter, or knife, cut the dough into four even rectangles.

Step 2

Step 4

## PULLMANS

The Pullman loaf is often referred to as sandwich bread because its long, square-like shape is perfect for sandwiches. Pullman pans have lids to help create this uniformly shaped loaf. Traditionally these loaves are made from white flour, but you can substitute whole-wheat or grain, or do a combination of the two.

1.  Take an individual piece of dough and place it on a lightly floured work surface.
2.  Fold the top and bottom of the dough halfway toward each other. They should almost touch in the middle.
3.  Follow the same process for the sides. Fold both sides toward the middle where they should almost touch.
4.  Starting at the top, fold the dough into itself about one-third of the way down. Repeat this folding method while rolling the dough into a cylindrical shape; make sure to keep tension in the dough's surface area.
5.  Roll the dough a few times on the work surface to make sure the seam is sealed.
6.  Place the dough seam-side down into a lightly oiled Pullman pan.

Step 2-3

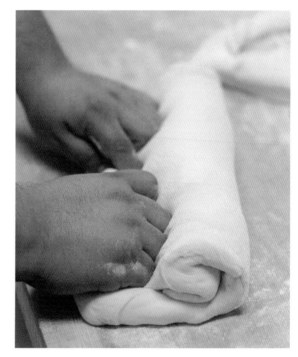

Step 4

## RUSTIC FREE-FORM

This shaping technique is for the most hydrated and artisan doughs. It is similar to the free-form oval, but this technique requires the least amount of handling, which is helpful because hydrated doughs are looser and can sometimes be difficult to manage.

1.  Take an individual piece of dough and place it on a lightly floured work surface.
2.  Fold both the top and bottom of the dough toward the middle, making sure the two edges meet.
3.  Press down on the seam very gently a few times to make sure it is sealed and that the dough has flattened slightly.
4.  Invert the dough.

Step 1

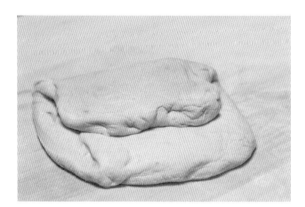

Step 2

Step 3

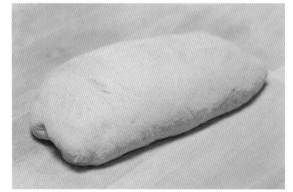

The shaped rustic free-form

**CHALLAH**

This braiding shaping technique will take a bit of practice to perfect. Don't get discouraged if you are not happy with your first efforts!

1. After chunking into 4 even pieces, take 1 piece and divide into 3 even pieces. Then divide each piece in half again. You should be left with 6 even pieces from each of the original 4 large chunked pieces.

2. Take each of these 6 pieces and roll it out into a long rope, approximately 12 inches (30 cm) long.

3. Make sure each strand is the same width throughout.

4. Pinch the top of the 6 strands together.

5. Separate 3 strands to the left and 3 to the right.

6. Move the innermost right strand straight up.

7. Take the left most strand and go over remaining 3 strands.

8. Bring the top strand back down.

9. Take the second inner right strand and bring over the strand you just brought down.

10. Continue this process with the rightmost strand until you have reached the bottom of the loaf.

11. Pinch the ends of the strand together.

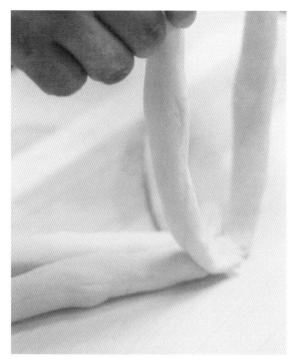

Step 4

Step 7

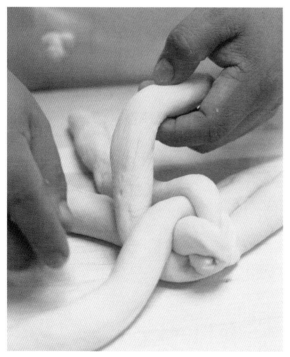

Step 9

Step 10

## DINNER ROLLS

1. Put a small chunk of dough on a lightly floured work surface. (Marble or wood is ideal.)

2. Gently roll between the palm of your hand and the work surface until round.

Note: as you get better at this, try to use both hands so you can shape two rolls at once.

 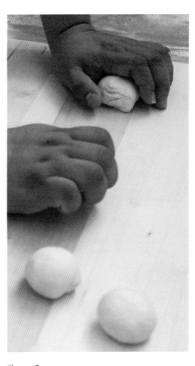 

Step 1                          Step 2                          The shaped rolls

## RUSTIC ROLLS

1. Use dough scraper to cut pieces of dough to weight specified in recipe.
2. Try and keep shapes uniform and sizing even when creating dough chunks, as the idea is to handle the dough as little as possible.

Step 1

## WHEN DO I GLAZE MY DOUGH AND ADD ANY EXTRA FINISHING TOUCHES?

Some breads require glazing or extra ingredients sprinkled on top after they have been shaped and proofed. Generally this takes place before baking, although some recipes may call for this step to be done postbaking. With challahs, brioches, and bagels, you should apply the egg glaze to the dough before baking. In some cases, recipes may call for sprinkling sesame or poppy seeds, or other types of seeds or spices. These should be sprinkled on after the glaze so that they stick.

# STEP 9: PROOFING

Proofing is the term used to describe the amount of time the dough stays out to rise *after* shaping. This is the final stage of the second fermentation period, and is the last chance for the dough to gain the bulk of its flavor. This is also when the dough finishes its final rise before baking. Proofing can take place in many different types of containers as long as the dough is covered so the surface skin is protected and stays soft and moist. If the skin isn't covered, it will dry out and hinder the rise and oven spring, or the rising that you want to achieve during baking. When time is not a factor, ideally, proofing should be done at room temperature, as the same concerns for the dough temperature that were mentioned earlier apply here. Dough proofing in a hot environment will rise much faster than dough proofing in a cooler environment. If time is a factor, finding a warmer place to rest your dough will accelerate proofing.

To determine whether or not your dough is ready to be baked, test it by touching the side with your fingertip. Similar to a memory foam mattress that retains the shape of your body, if the dough retains an indentation from your finger, then it is ready to be baked. If not, it needs more time to proof.

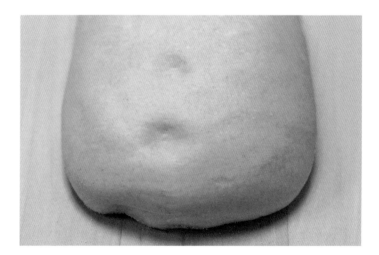

The Finger Test

# HOW DO YOU SCORE BREAD AND WHY?

To score the bread means to cut into the top of the dough (with a knife or a sterile razor blade) after it rises (postproofing) but before putting it in the oven. The purpose of scoring is to release some of the still-trapped carbon dioxide, while offering the bread an aesthetically pleasing look. In the oven, the bread will be both expanding and forming a crust at the same time. In general, without scores on the top of the loaf, the crust will form more of a shell, not allowing the bread to bake or expand equally in all directions. However, not all breads need to be scored. For example, most breads made in pans, like Pullmans, and softer breads like challah do not need to be scored. Hearth breads like baguettes, ryes, and sourdoughs should be scored before they are baked.

When scoring the bread, make sure to be gentle and cut sharply rather than in a continuous motion to avoid tearing the dough. The cut should be thin as it will expand when in the oven. You can score dough with a razor blade or a sharp kitchen knife, serrated or straight. As long as you are cutting at an angle and your cuts are clean, the scoring should expand properly in the oven, as well as offer an aesthetically pleasing look to your finished loaf.

## A SIMPLE TEST FOR OVEN HOT SPOTS?

To find the hot spots in your oven, you can also perform what is commonly known as the "bread test," in which you cover a baking sheet with slices of white bread (commercial sandwich bread is fine) and heat them up at 350°F (175°C) for a few minutes. When they are done, you will notice that some spots are burnt while others are toasted perfectly. The burnt spots mark the location of the hot spots in your oven.

## WHAT DO YOU DO IF YOUR OVEN DOESN'T REACH THE RECOMMENDED HIGH TEMPERATURES?

If you are working with an oven that doesn't reach the highest temperatures suggested in these recipes, it would be helpful to invest in a baking or pizza stone. The stone absorbs and then radiates the heat out, thus increasing the overall temperature in the oven and of the dough itself if it is baking directly on the stone. This is an inexpensive fix that will allow you to capture more heat in your oven and improve the crust on your finished loaf.

# STEP 10: BAKING

What actually happens during baking that turns the fermented dough into something delicious to eat? The heat causes several chemical reactions and processes to occur while the bread is baking, transforming it into food we can ingest. The heat causes what is commonly known as the "oven spring" by forcing gas cells in the dough to expand. Secondly, the heat causes the yeast to become inactive—the live yeast will be killed at such high temperatures. Next, caramelization of the natural and added sugars occurs, as the crust begins to form. This means that the heat causes the sugar molecules to change color, turning golden brown. Overbaking will lead to the blackening of these sugar molecules, a mistake commonly known as burning your bread. Finally, the actual crust is formed when the starches on the outer layer of the bread gelatinize—meaning, because of the heat, the starch molecules absorb as much moisture as they can find and therefore swell until they can swell no more. And then they explode. The water that has been absorbed thickens because of the starch, creating a liquid-like gelatin coating that hardens into a crispy crust. Gelatinization isn't complete until the temperature reaches approximately 200°F (95°C), and can only occur when moisture is present.

As discussed earlier, one of the most important things to become familiar with is your oven. After all, if the kitchen is in essence a lab, then the oven is the Bunsen burner, and it must be used with precision and skill. How accurate is your oven's temperature gauge? Does it have any hot or cold spots, and if so, where are they? Don't make the mistake of assuming that the temperature gauge on the oven is accurate; many oven gauges are not—and even the most expensive ovens have their idiosyncrasies. It will take some trial and error to figure out how to best navigate these deficiencies and produce the ideal results.

Using an oven thermometer will help you determine whether or not your oven is at the correct temperature, as well as help you sniff out some of the hot and cold spots. You should also be prepared to rotate the bread 180 degrees halfway through the allotted baking time to ensure an even bake. By rotating the bread's placement in the oven, you can attempt to compensate for any hot spots that do exist. You can also use a baking stone, as mentioned and explained earlier, to even out the heat in your oven and bake the bread more consistently.

## CREATING STEAM

Creating steam in the oven while it preheats has many benefits for the finished loaf. It keeps the inside of the oven moist, making sure the dough doesn't dry out while giving the final loaf a shiny exterior. It also allows the bread to rise faster, and is necessary in order for the crust to form, as previously mentioned. It is important to note that the presence of steam is only needed during the first part of the baking process in order to gelatinize the crust and give it that sheen. The second half of baking requires a drier environment for the newly formed crust to become crispy and hard.

To create steam in the oven, place a shallow pan filled about halfway with water on the bottom rack of the oven while it preheats. Spray bottles of water can also be used during baking. Carefully spray the sides of the oven to increase the amount of steam created. Once the oven has reached the desired temperature, you should remove the pan of water. The purpose is to create steam, but not a constant source of steam. If there is too much steam your bread will still be acceptable, but it will not achieve the artisan crust you are aspiring to. Instead it will have a strange shiny crust that will lack crisp and crunch. At Orwashers, we have dampers in our commercial ovens to relieve some of the steam during the last ten minutes of the baking time in order to compensate for the humidity that is already in the air. Since average kitchen ovens are much smaller than those in a bakery, dampers aren't necessary for home baking.

## TESTING THE BREAD

How can you tell if the bread is done baking? There are a few ways you can determine whether or not your bread is done baking—some are more exact than others. If you want to take the more scientific route, you can take the temperature of the inside of your loaf of bread. Fully baked bread will have an internal temperature of around 200°F (93°C). Bear in mind that the outside of the bread will be much hotter than the inside since it is directly exposed to the heat inside the oven. Softer breads and breads with additional fats like brioches and challahs may have internal temperatures that are a little lower than 200°F (93°C), while heartier breads like sourdoughs will fall closer to that target. Use your digital thermometer to test the temperature of your bread by inserting it into the center of your loaf, from the bottom up. This way you won't ruin the presentation of your loaf. If you are baking in a pan, take the loaf out of the pan to insert the thermometer in the bottom. If it isn't done, simply place the loaf back into the pan and bake for a few more minutes.

If you don't have a thermometer, or would rather not poke a hole in your loaf, you can simply turn the loaf of bread over and tap the bottom of it gently with your thumb. Again, if you are baking in a pan, you will have to take the loaf out to perform this test. If the sound your thumb makes is hollow, your bread is done. If it sounds thicker and more like a foot stomp, then it needs more time in the oven. If you have never performed this test before, you should begin to test the dough before the time is up purposely, when you know the bread isn't ready, so you can hear what it sounds like when it isn't hollow. Continue testing every fifteen minutes or so until you can hear a discernible difference between taps and have achieved the hollow sound you are hoping for.

Additionally, you can—and should—use visual clues, no matter what other tests or methods you employ. Even if a loaf of bread has reached an internal temperature of 200°F (93°C), that doesn't necessarily mean it is done baking. There are many factors that play into how the bread bakes, including the idiosyncrasies of your oven, how much moisture is surrounding the loaf, and how the dough fermented, to name just a few. Some breads will reach internal temperatures higher than 210°F (99°C) and still not be finished baking. That said, you should always look at the loaf and pay attention to the color of the crust. If the crust is still very pale and white looking, the bread isn't done yet. The sugar and gluten in the bread still need time to caramelize to give you that beautiful, golden brown crust.

Time is also an important factor. The more bread you bake, the more familiar you will become with your oven and how quickly or slowly it works. In time, you will be able to determine how long a loaf of bread needs to bake in your oven—even if that time differs from what is advised in the recipe. The key is learning how to read the cues that show your bread is done rather than slavishly following recipe baking times.

The perfectly baked loaf is measured by temperature, how it looks and how it sounds when tapped.

# STEP 11: COOLING

It is a common misconception that baking is the final step in the process of bread baking. Many people assume that eating a piece of bread fresh from the oven is the best possible way to eat bread, but they would be mistaken. Even when bread is done baking, it is not ready to be eaten—yet. A loaf of bread must cool properly after baking; otherwise, it won't fully achieve its potential. Cooling for a period of time brings the bread's temperature down from its typical 200°F (93°C) on the inside—and hotter on the outside—to room temperature, which usually falls somewhere around 70°F (21°C). Artisan bread, once baked, can take anywhere from two to five hours to cool down to room temperature. Some bakers leave their breads cooling overnight, or even sitting out for a day or two. The time it takes to sufficiently cool a loaf of bread is subject to preference, as well as the type of bread being made.

What happens during the cooling process? Several things are still taking place inside the walls of the crust even though the bread is no longer baking. At this point in the process, the starches are still setting. The significant amount of moisture that the starch molecules absorbed during baking needs time to evaporate. If you slice into a loaf of bread fresh out of the oven, the crumb will feel sticky, gummy, and even wet, because you have not let enough time pass for the moisture to leave the loaf. For this reason, you should not store your bread until it has fully cooled. There is also a significant amount of flavor still forming at this stage, so keep that in mind as well.

Once the bread is done baking, you should transfer it to a wire cooling rack as quickly as possible. A wire rack is ideal for two reasons: First, moving the bread off the pan or rack it originally baked on ensures that the bread will not keep baking on a hot surface. Second, the holes in the wire rack ensure that all sides of the bread will cool evenly. Unlike many other stages in this process, the bread should remain uncovered while it cools. The air circulation will allow the moisture molecules to evaporate from the bread into the atmosphere. If the bread doesn't cool in an open space, the moisture will not be able to escape and the bread will become soggy.

*Orwashers Artisan Bread*

There is no exact amount of time that bread should cool for. The loose guide is that bread should be eaten at room temperature, so you should at least wait until then to cut into your loaf. However, many breads continue to develop flavor as they sit out, and therefore will benefit from waiting longer before wrapping and storing. For example, sourdough bread traditionally tastes better at least one full day after baking. Rye breads typically need even longer to develop their final taste. Knowing how long to let a particular loaf or type of bread sit takes some educated guessing coupled with experience. Feel free to experiment; if you are baking two loaves of the same type of bread, leave one to cool till it's room temperature and then taste a piece. Leave the other to cool a few hours longer, or even overnight, and then try that loaf. See if you can discern the differences in flavor and/ or consistency. Decide for yourself which one you like better and use that as a time gauge for that type of bread moving forward.

Determining whether or not a loaf of bread has reached room temperature is fairly intuitive. Simply cup your hands around the outside of the bread. If it still feels warm, it needs to cool a little longer. If this is your first time baking bread or cooling, you can check the temperature every thirty to forty-five minutes after taking it out of the oven to help you get a sense for the changing temperature and how quickly or slowly the bread is cooling.

# STEP 12: STORING

Artisan breads will usually only last up to two or three days after they have been baked. If you would like to give your loaf a longer life, there are ways of storing it to preserve it better. Bread should always be kept out of direct sunlight and instead, stored in a dark, cool place, to avoid condensation and the eventual growing of mold and bacteria.

If you have a breadbox in your kitchen, this is the best place to store your bread. If not, there are other ways to preserve your loaves. Lean breads are best stored in paper bags that are sealed at the top if they are going to be

*Orwashers Artisan Bread*

left out at room temperature. The loaves can be sliced or unsliced. The paper allows the bread to breathe a little, which is good for the starches, while keeping the crust intact. Plastic will create moisture that will cause the crust to lose its crunch. Beware, however, that bread stored at room temperature will only last for about a day if it is sitting out. For longer-term storage, you can freeze lean breads, but they will not retain the same texture and crispness in their crusts. If you are going to freeze a lean bread, wrap it in plastic wrap or tin foil all the way around so that no air can get inside it, and then store it in an airtight plastic bag. Make sure to deflate all the air from the bag before placing the bread in the freezer. You can do this with an uncut loaf or a sliced loaf, but note that sliced bread will not defrost the same way as an uncut loaf. An unsliced loaf will defrost and keep its texture if you give it enough time to do so before consuming it (generally at least 2-3 hours). If you sliced the loaf before freezing it, you will have to toast it after freezing to try to regain the texture and flavor. Enriched breads should be wrapped in plastic wrap or tin foil, sealed in plastic bags, and frozen for long-term storage. Because these breads are moister than lean breads, the plastic helps them retain their moisture. But they should not be left out at room temperature for too long in plastic because they will become a breeding ground for mold. Bread keeps well in the freezer anywhere from one week to three weeks depending on the type of bread and how well it is packaged.

You may be tempted to store your bread in the refrigerator instead of the freezer, but you should avoid this. While it might seem like a shortcut to defrosting, it will actually cause your bread to grow stale faster. The cold, wet environment of the refrigerator causes the starch cells in the bread to crystallize, meaning that they absorb whatever moisture is left in the bread and in the air, traps it, and crystallizes it so it hardens. This makes the crust more rigid, and causes the crumb to harden and become stale.

If you've read all twelve steps carefully, you're ready to graduate from Baking 101, gather your ingredients, and begin crafting your own artisan breads.

## WHAT IS A BREADBOX AND HOW DOES IT WORK?

There are a lot of different breadboxes on the market, and they can be made from a variety of materials, including wood, plastic, and metal. A breadbox creates a controlled environment for your bread that falls somewhere in between a paper bag and a plastic bag, so to speak. It allows some moisture to enter but not too much so the bread will get soggy or moldy, and it allows the bread to breathe enough so that the crust will stay crunchy. Breadboxes can preserve a fresh loaf of bread for up to three days.

# Chapter 3

# Ingredients And The Local Movement

One of the aspects of my role as a baker and a bakery owner, and a particular passion of mine, is the process of procuring our ingredients. When I took over Orwashers, I vowed to reemphasize the importance of having pure, natural, local ingredients in our breads, and the result is healthier, heartier, tastier bread. This is why I like to use the flour that Kevin Richardson produces from North Country Mills. The way he mills his white flour leaves in a good amount of bran and germ. It is stone ground and that imparts a great flavor, texture, and hydration level to my breads (more about Kevin and North Country Mills on page 100). Farmer Ground Flour, is another grower and miller that I like. Located in Trumansburg, New York, the wheat they produce tastes amazing, and I love that their flour is produced the old-fashioned way. I suspect that the local flour I source today is much closer to the kind of flour the bakery was baking with when it first opened its doors.

The difference between eating bread baked from fresh, local wheat flour and bread that was baked from long-term packaged, store-bought flour is similar to the difference between eating a Florida orange freshly picked from the tree in the grove and eating a Florida orange you buy in a grocery store weeks after it has been picked. Because local flour and commercial flour are different, local flour needs to be treated differently during baking. Adjustments to yeast and water measurements, as well as baking times, may need to be made to compensate for the strain of local flour that is grown in your area and other factors such as weather conditions. These are things you will learn over time should you decide to use locally grown flour.

Most people don't know that local flour has a different genealogy than common commercial flour. But in order to understand the difference, we first must learn what flour is and where it comes from.

Flour is milled from wheat grains. Wheat in its natural from-the-farm form is known as wheat berry. The wheat berry has three basic parts: the endosperm, the germ, and the bran. The germ drives the growth of the wheat, and accounts for only 2 to 3 percent of the total berry. This part is also rich in oil and vitamin E. The endosperm serves as the food for the growing germ and accounts for about 75 percent of the berry; it is rich with protein and nutrients. The bran is the hard outside

*"Using pure, natural, local ingredients in our breads results in healthier, heartier, tastier bread."*

*Orwashers Artisan Bread*

layer that acts as protection for the tiny germ. White flour is milled of almost entirely endosperm, while whole-wheat flour includes all three parts. Locally grown flour is much closer to the flour of our ancestors; it has not been crossbred or modified like commercial flours. This means the flour is natural and unaltered; it is not a cross between two strains, nor is it bleached or otherwise stripped of any of its parts and nutrients. For this reason, local flour tastes better than store-bought flour. It is also much fresher than flour that has been grown elsewhere, imported, and packaged for bulk consumption.

Local flour is usually produced in small, local mills, which will generally be stone-ground mills, whereas larger commercial millers are roller mills. In stone-ground mills, the process by which the grain is milled leaves the whole grain intact, and therefore the grain retains most of its nutrients and nutty flavor. Roller mills, on the other hand, were designed for efficiency in our modern times, and strip the grain to try and coax as much "white" flour as possible from it. The process allows them to produce a lot more white flour, and to do so faster. However, your bread will pay the price in taste.

Despite all the positives of using stone-ground flour from small mills, we still face challenges working with local ingredients from a wholesale perspective. Local flour varies more from season to season; therefore, getting the hydration perfect during baking for a consistent product can be challenging. There are several factors contributing to variances in the flour: crop year; which mill grinds the flour; whether the flour is stone ground or goes through a roller mill; and lastly, how long the flour is stored from the time it is milled until the time you use it. For example, we received an order of flour that had been recently milled on newly sharpened stones with less than a week of aging. We were experimenting with a particular style of bread, and while previous experiments went well, this flour yielded a dough that looked like soup. Our hydration rates, while perfect two weeks earlier, were out of whack with this particular batch of flour and so we had to make additional adjustments. But, in the end, I believe that using local flour produces results that are well worth the effort.

## MILLSTONE VERSUS A ROLLER MILL

When wheat grains are ground on a millstone, the whole grain is used—that means all three of its parts. The whole grain is placed between two circular stones and ground through once. It retains all the nutrients and flavors that the grain started with. This is the way millers have been grinding wheat since flour was first created. Roller mills use metal scrapers instead of stone to strip the grain layer by layer to extract the lighter parts of the grain, what would become white flour. You can get commercial whole-wheat flour, as it is now possible to enrich or add the nutrients back in to the grains that have gone through the roller mill, but it won't be the same as stone-ground whole-wheat.

# THE SIX CLASSES
# OF WHEAT GRAINS

The type of flour you end up with depends on the grain you are starting with. There are hundreds of different grains of wheat grown in the United States, and many of them are used to make the flour we bake with today. Some grains are grown in the Midwest, while others are more particular to the Northeast. Where each wheat grain grows best is based on soil conditions, climate, rainfall, and sometimes custom.

The strains of wheat grown in the United States are divided into six classes. The categories of division are based on several criteria: when they are planted and harvested, what color they are, their consistency, and their shape. In general, softer wheat strains are lower in protein than harder wheat strains, which is helpful to know when choosing flour for bread baking. The higher the protein content, the more gluten in the flour. Within these six classes of wheat, there are hundreds of different specific types of wheat. It is quite common for millers to mix more than one kind of wheat together when making a particular type of flour, and the chances are the flour you buy in your local grocery store will contain a combination of several of these types of wheat.

## HARD RED WINTER

This strain of wheat is great for all-purpose flours. It has a wide range of uses—due in part to its range in protein content—including baking sweets as well as breads, and rolls in particular. It is red in color. This wheat is the most produced in the United States and its dominant wheat export. Winter wheat is planted before it freezes in the winter, and is harvested in the summer.

## HARD RED SPRING

Hard Red Spring wheat is ideal for artisan breads since it has the highest protein content, with ranges of 13 percent to 16 percent. It is a great wheat for bread flour, and is also often used as a blending wheat for other types of flour in order to increase the overall protein content. It is planted in the spring and harvested in the fall.

## SOFT RED WINTER

This strain is low in protein, so it is better for cookies than it is for bread, which benefits from more gluten. Soft Red Winter wheat is also used for crackers and other flat breads. It is planted in the winter and harvested in the summer.

## SOFT WHITE WHEAT

This wheat is primarily grown in the Pacific Northwest, and has a traditionally low protein content, making it best for cakes and pastries. It has a softer and milder taste than hard wheat.

## HARD WHITE WHEAT

This is the newest class of wheat. It is similar to Hard Red Winter Wheat, only whiter in color. It is higher in protein, approximately 10 to 12 percent, so it is good for pan breads and whole-wheat, but is also great for lighter colored breads like French bread.

## DURUM

This wheat strain has a very high protein percentage of up to 15 percent, but durum flour doesn't produce gluten bonds the way other flours do. The gluten bonds formed by durum flour are less extensible than bread or all-purpose flour. This strain of wheat is primarily used for pasta, as it is the hardest of all six classes.

*There are hundreds of different kinds of wheat grown in the U.S.*

# THE BASIC TYPES OF FLOUR

From many different types of wheat, many kinds of flour are made and you will have a selection available to you in your local supermarket. Although I strongly recommend getting your flour from local millers if possible, you may use store-bought versions of any of these flours below to make the recipes in this book. This section will help explain the basic types of flour that are used in bread baking and their main differences.

First we need to discuss some terms that apply to all types of flour: regular, organic, and enriched. By regular flour, I am referring to the average flour you purchase at your local grocery store. Mass-produced flour can be lacking in nutrients, depending on what kind you buy, and may have some added chemicals and preservatives.

Enriched flour is flour that has had nutrients and vitamins infused back into the flour after the milling process. Since many mills will strip the wheat grains of the germ and the berry, which is where the nutrients live, flour producers will enrich their flour by adding nutrients like niacin, thiamine and riboflavin.

Organic flour is the most natural flour you can purchase, as well as being the healthiest for you. This means the flour has been processed without using any genetic modifications, and has followed the organic guidelines for chemicals and pesticides. Most organic mills will also retain as much of the natural nutrients and vitamins from the wheat grain as possible. Clearly, this is the best choice for your bread baking.

## WHAT IS THE DIFFERENCE BETWEEN BLEACHED AND UNBLEACHED FLOUR?

Unbleached flour is white wheat flour in its natural form. This means it retains a natural yellow tint from the beta-carotene that exists in the grain. This nutrient also contributes to flour's nutty smell. Although it is more yellow in color than white, it is still considered white flour.

Bleached white flour has been bleached with chemicals to take away its natural yellow tint, which is what gives it a pure white color. Bleached flour will also lack the traditional wheaty aroma.

You can have bleached and unbleached in different varieties, including white flour, white whole-wheat flour, bread flour, and all-purpose flour, to name a few. It is always preferable to use unbleached flour, if you can find it. Be sure to read the label. As a general rule, if the package doesn't say "unbleached," you should assume it is bleached.

White flour, while very popular in mainstream baking today, is definitely lacking in health benefits because it's refined in such a way that it doesn't retain most of the nutrients from the grain. White whole-wheat flour is a good compromise: mild flavor and taste but all the nutrition of whole wheat.

## WHITE FLOUR

White flour is made from hard white wheat. These wheat grains are heavily processed and refined so they don't retain much of the germ or bran parts of the wheat grain, which in turn means they lose much of the wheat grains' natural nutrients and vitamins. White flour is traditionally lower in fiber content and protein than bread flour, and usually falls somewhere between 8 and 10 percent. You can get white flour in a variety of forms, including bleached and unbleached. White flour is best for lighter breads that aren't too yeast heavy, like focaccia.

## ALL-PURPOSE FLOUR (PLAIN FLOUR)

All-purpose flour is a type of white flour that can be used for anything from bread to piecrusts. It is usually made from two different strains of wheat, and has a protein content of around 10 to 12 percent. This is a great choice for bread baking if you don't have any bread flour; but since it has a lower gluten percentage than bread flour, be aware that your bread might be slightly less dense or elastic than it otherwise would be. Still, if you have a bag of all-purpose flour at your disposal, I would suggest using it all up first before experimenting with bread and other types of flour. Your bread will still be delicious!

## WHITE WHOLE-WHEAT FLOUR

White whole-wheat flour is milled from hard white spring wheat. It has many of the same qualities as all-purpose flour and unbleached white flour, including a milder color, taste, and aroma, but it has the all the nutrition of whole wheat. This can be a great substitution for white flour; it will give you healthier bread without the added density and earthy flavors of whole wheat.

## WHOLE-WHEAT FLOUR

Whole-wheat flour is milled using the whole-wheat grain: germ, endosperm, and bran. It has a traditionally nutty flavor and will create denser dough that is a little bit sweet. It is also high in nutrients and fiber. You can find whole-wheat flour in regular and organic versions; commercial whole-wheat flour still extracts a good amount of nutrients, however, so I always advise buying organic whenever possible.

The germ and bran parts of the wheat are present in whole-wheat flour and give it texture and a brownish color.

## BREAD FLOUR

There is an important distinction between bread flour and all-purpose flour when baking bread. All-purpose flour has a lower protein percentage since its intended use is generic. Bread flour has a slightly higher percentage of protein (typically around 14 percent). This makes it the most ideal choice for bread baking because it adds to the extensibility and elasticity of the dough and allows the dough to rise more easily. (There are nuanced differences in flavor between the two types of flour, but both are perfectly acceptable for bread.) I prefer this type of flour for bread baking, unless the recipe specifically calls for something else. It is perfect for almost all types of bread, from challah to sourdough to rye, offering the bread strong gluten bonds for great elasticity and the perfect oven rise. Like other flours, bread flour also comes in different varieties. My preference is always unbleached and organic bread flour, if you can find it. However, it is perfectly fine to use all-purpose flour if you don't have bread flour.

## SPRING FLOUR

Spring flour is made from spring wheat, which is a hard wheat that is mostly grown in the Great Plains. Spring wheat is planted in the spring and harvested in the summer. It produces a slightly reddish color, as opposed to a golden one. Hard wheat is high in protein, so it's great to use spring flour for all yeast breads.

There are different kinds of rye flour and the color will depend on the part of the rye berry that is milled. This dark rye flour gets its color from the outer parts of the rye berry.

## RYE AND RYE FLOUR

Throughout Orwashers history, Jewish rye bread has been a staple and a symbol of the bakery. And, as such, it will always be something that we make with pride. Even though my focus was on adding international breads when I took over the bakery, there were some New York institutions that I felt compelled to stay true to—and two of those staples were the rye bread and the pumpernickel bread. What would the pastrami sandwich be without a tangy rye bread studded with caraway seeds? How can you imagine serving smoked fish on anything other than pumpernickel?

Rye is a hardy grain that is known for being much more resilient in the field than wheat. Rye can sustain itself during floods as well as survive during times of drought. In fact, rye has been deemed the "poverty grain" because it is often grown in soil that would be too unfruitful for other grain varieties. Due to this fact, rye's popularity increased in countries with particularly cold climates. Nordic ryes found in Germany and Denmark are traditionally very hearty and dark with thick crusts. It makes sense that the New York–style rye bread we enjoy today was inspired by the traditions of Eastern European immigrants, which blends in some lighter wheat flour as well.

Rye flour is known for being higher in fiber and much drier than wheat flour. And rye flour contains much less gluten than wheat flour does. This affects rye breads in two ways. The gluten networks that form during fermentation produce carbon dioxide that helps to trap air bubbles in the dough. This allows the dough to rise. Without as much gluten, the rye dough has fewer air bubbles. This is what gives rye bread its characteristically dense property. Secondly, rye has a higher content of naturally occurring sugars than does wheat. The higher the sugar content in a given dough, the faster it will ferment. This is something that must be accounted for when baking with rye flour.

There are several types of rye breads: light rye, dark rye, marble rye, and pumpernickel, to name a few. They all differ based on what parts of the rye berry—the portion of the grain that gets ground—were used to make the flour. The outer parts of the rye berry contain more pigments, and it is these parts that are used to make the darker loaves. Pumpernickel is made by grinding whole rye berries into what's known as pumpernickel flour.

To counter the rye's intrinsically dry properties, bakers in Nordic countries will soak the entire rye berry in water for several hours before mixing, and eventually baking, their traditional one hundred percent rye bread. You may recall that in Chapter 2, I mentioned the potential for presoaking grains. This is a perfect example of when this process of presoaking comes in handy. It is because of rye's natural dryness that you will often see rye bread recipes calling for a rye and wheat blend, which is the way the New York Rye from Orwashers is baked. It makes for a slightly moister loaf, but one that is no doubt equally delicious whether eaten alone or with pastrami!

## HOW DIFFERENT TYPES OF FLOUR REACT TO WATER

As mentioned earlier, different types and brands of flour will react to water differently. Some flours absorb more water than others. Depending on what kind of flour you choose and who the manufacturer is, you may have nutrition information—including the protein percentage—available to you, either on the company's website or on the back of the packaging. Supplying this information has become much more common among artisan flour producers. Higher protein flours have a higher gluten content, and therefore they absorb more water. This will cause your crumb structure to be tighter, and cause the crust to be a bit more elastic. Bagels and pizza dough often use higher protein flours, to give you a point of reference. Higher protein flour also allows more room for error when you are mixing. If you overmix a dough with high protein flour, your final product may not be the perfect loaf you had hoped for, but it will still be okay. Lower protein flours are not as forgiving when you overmix. Your final product will be tough and may not rise the way you would want it to.

## SPELT

Spelt is an ancient grain that is a cousin to wheat. Recently, spelt flour has been reclaimed by the general public because of its reputation for being much lower in gluten and higher in protein than wheat. Spelt flour does not absorb as much water as wheat flour, and therefore requires a lower hydration when baking. Breads baked with spelt flour often have a nutty and earthy essence. The spelt bread we bake at Orwashers has quinoa, raisins, sunflower seeds, and honey in it to form a dense and moist loaf with a touch of sweetness that is also very healthy. It is a great alternative for people with gluten allergies.

## BUCKWHEAT

Buckwheat is not wheat or a grain, but rather a wide-spreading, flowering plant that produces seeds, which can be milled into a flour. Buckwheat is renowned for its health benefits, since it is naturally gluten-free, and is high in protein, amino acids, and soluble fiber.

OPPOSITE PAGE Potato flour has a more granular texture than white or whole-wheat flour, which is more powdery.

## POTATOES AND POTATO FLOUR

Potatoes can be made into an incredibly useful flour for a variety of different types of bread. In addition to being gluten-free, potatoes are a source of fiber, B-vitamins, potassium, and iron. Potato flour attracts and retains water, which adds moisture and creates a light, delicate crumb. Potato flour is a go-to choice for burger buns, and that's exactly how we make our buns at Orwashers. The potato flour gives our buns a light, fluffy, and slightly sweeter dough that will not dry out easily, making them a favorite amongst our staff and our customer base!

# THE LOCAL MOVEMENT

While flour is the main and most important ingredient in your bread, it pays to search out local sources for the other ingredients as well. If you're making bread that calls for eggs, I recommend using farm-fresh, local organic eggs. Farm-fresh eggs are healthier and tastier than the alternative. The chickens are free-range, which means they are allowed as much fresh air and exercise as they desire, and they are fed fresh vegetation without any chemicals.

The same goes for milk—use organic and/or local milk if you can find it. Whole milk is the ideal type to give your bread the right taste and texture. Milk makes your bread fluffier, softer, and richer tasting, so it stands to reason that you would want the very best you can find.

As you can see, I believe strongly in the local movement for food. Why are local ingredients so important? Local food is always healthier for you because crops begin to lose nutrients from the moment they are harvested. The sooner you can eat them, the more health benefits you receive. The farther food has to travel—and the more processes of preservation and packaging it needs to sustain that travel—the less nutritious it will be at the time of consumption. Food that is eaten when it's fresh also tastes better, as you have surely gathered from experience.

Another reason I support local farmers and millers and use locally grown ingredients whenever possible is because I believe it is good for the economy of the community where one lives. On a global level, producers of organic, locally grown food care deeply about healthy food and work toward that end. Farmer Ground Flour, for example, also works closely with the Northeast Organic Farming Association (NOFA) and Northeast Organic Wheat Project in their efforts to create the best tasting and best performing products for local artisans.

However, I wouldn't be doing any favors to these farmers who are working so hard to bring back the wheat industry if I didn't use their products to make breads that would appeal—and of course, sell—to the masses. While I do my best to source our ingredients locally, there are some ingredients that are difficult to grow here in New York. Therefore, at Orwashers we tend to use a mixture of local and commercial ingredients, but even our commercial ingredients are always held to the highest quality standards. You should keep that guiding principle in mind—choose local, choose the best quality you can find—to ensure that the bread you'll be baking will be the best tasting, best-for-you bread that you can make.

There are a large variety of grains available, which will produce distinctly different flavors in your bread.

# BECOMING PART OF THE LOCAL FOOD MOVEMENT

Cities and towns all over the country are turning to local ingredients for healthy, quality products. If you're interested in finding local farms and farmer's markets in your area, there are organizations that can help you.

**LOCAL HARVEST** is a nationwide organic and local food website that specializes in finding local and organic food sources for the public. www.localharvest.org

**NATIONAL SUSTAINABLE INFORMATION SERVICE** is an organization that provides information on sustainable agriculture. The organization provide a local food directory on its website. www.attra.ncat.org

**THE UNITED STATES DEPARTMENT OF AGRICULTURE** provides useful information on its website, including a list of national farmer's markets. www.ams.usda.gov/AMSv1.0/farmersmarkets

**THE ORGANIC CONSUMERS ASSOCIATION** is an online nonprofit that advocates for health and sustainability. It has a green buyers guide listed on its website. www.organicconsumers.org/btc/BuyingGuide.cfm

**FOOD ROUTES** is a nationwide organization that offers support, networking, and informational resources to local organizations hoping to rebuild sustainable food systems. They offer a section on their website about how to buy local food products. www.foodroutes.org

**THE EAT WELL GUIDE** allows you to find healthy, organic food anywhere so you can eat well on the go. www.eatwellguide.org

*"When I hear the term "artisan," I think of old-world quality. If I see that word, I know the producer cares and the quality is there."*

-Kevin Richardson

Supporting other like-minded artisans is extremely important to me. At Orwashers, we work with other local companies, like Brooklyn pickle maker Rick's Picks and Hudson Valley jam maker Beth's Farm Kitchen. It gives me great pride to offer these locally made products at Orwashers; I feel that I am part of the process of keeping our local economy alive and well, while offering people truly quality products that I know they will enjoy.

*Ingredients and The Local Movement*

## BAKER KEITH AND KEVIN RICHARDSON, OWNER OF NORTH COUNTRY MILLS

I've been working with Kevin for a little over three years. Part of what attracted me to his company was that they are dedicated and committed to growing "the best." They are very selective with their grains, and are particular about flavor and crop performance. We have worked together closely to determine what the best kinds of wheat are for different kinds of bread, based on a variety of important factors such as how the flour will absorb water, how well it rises, and of course, its flavor. They offer many different types of flour including high-extraction bread flour (or "half-white" flour), whole-wheat flour, all-purpose flour, and rye flour. The process of working with North Country Mills has been a real collaboration, and I love being a part of the process from the ground up. It's incredible to be able to play a role in how the wheat gets grown and milled, and to offer up my experience and expertise when it comes to the ways the wheat ultimately bakes and tastes.

North Country Mills takes pride in growing grains that are particularly suited to artisan breads.

## Q&A WITH FARMER AND MILLER KEVIN RICHARDSON:

### HOW DID YOU COME TO WORK WITH KEITH AND ORWASHERS?

When I started North Country Farms in 2008, I started small, building my brand around bakers here in upstate New York. Once the model was proven, I made a trip to New York City and started knocking on doors of artisan bread bakers. Keith responded very quickly after testing my sample. We began working together in the summer of 2010.

### TELL US ABOUT YOUR MILL. WHAT MAKES YOUR PROCESS DIFFERENT FROM OTHER MILLS?

Our grain is sourced, produced, and sold all within a 350-mile radius. We mill grain with stones, and today this style of milling is unique. We grind at low temperatures, allowing our flour to contain the grain's full nutritional value when bagged. How do we ensure this? We base our quality control on temperature. No wheat passing through our mill is ground over 140°F (60°C). Unlike us, high processed mills grind their grains at such high temperatures that the grain loses all nutritional value in the product. This is why you will see a long list of added enrichments and preservatives. Our flour is completely natural. It has no added enrichment or preserves. The fact that we source raw material within our own region and we grind 100 percent of our grains with stone makes for a high quality product that not many companies offer in the Northeast.

## WHAT WAS THE PROCESS OF FINDING THE PERFECT PRODUCT FOR KEITH LIKE? WHAT PRODUCTS OF YOURS DOES KEITH USE IN HIS BREAD?

We lucked out when Keith tested our product. It was a fairly simply transition. After sending him samples, we didn't have to do much. He was happy with the original product that we had been milling, at that point for approximately two years. Keith currently uses our Stone Ground White Bread Flour and is in the process of working with our whole-wheat.

## WHAT WAS WORKING WITH KEITH LIKE? WHAT DID YOU LEARN FROM THIS EXPERIENCE?

Keith is a great baker who offers a product that is none other than exquisite. Therefore, he expects the product he is putting into his bread to be the same. Consistency is important, and Keith thrives on consistent product. Keith has taught me that bringing quality product to market will sell. He has taught me to push through the tough times and always fix the problem. This is a competitive market, and there are other mills hoping to attract Keith's business. As a start-up miller/entrepreneur, the insight from Keith has been invaluable; it has pushed me to be very hands-on. His guidance through this process has helped me grow as a small mill, and with us working together we have grown with Orwashers.

## WHAT ARE YOUR THOUGHTS ON KEITH'S PHILOSOPHY OF LOCAL SOURCING?

Keith is reverting back to the way food used to be. He is doing what all bakers need to be doing: sourcing local, sourcing quality, and offering great products made with those ingredients. I immensely respect what he is doing. Because of outreach like this, our consumers are beginning to better understand the origin of foods, as well as becoming more aware of where their foods are coming from. Keith's customers know when they buy his breads, his ingredients are local and of the highest quality. This philosophy also keeps small local food businesses like mine operational.

## DO YOU SHARE KEITH'S PHILOSOPHY OF SUPPORTING LIKE-MINDED ARTISANS?

When I hear the term "artisan," I think of old-world quality. If I see that word, I know they care and the quality is there. I am proud to say that my flour is sold to numerous artisan bakers.

# Chapter 4

## Preferments: Starters, Levains, and Bigas

One of the most important aspects to baking artisanal breads that differs from the baking of commercial breads is the use of preferments, or starters. Preferments are live, active yeast cultures that are added to the dough to achieve complex flavors and irregular, aerated crumb structures and chewy crusts. We already know that the longer something ferments, the richer the flavors will be. Using a preferment, or a live yeast culture that has been active for longer than the dough you have mixed, helps to extend the fermentation of your dough as a whole, ultimately adding flavor. However, the tradeoff is that preferments require time and effort. Since they are live cultures, they need constant attention. But, if cared for under the correct conditions, preferments can be maintained for years.

There are two types of starters, stiff starters and liquid starters, and within these there are different kinds of stiff starters and different types of liquid starters. A stiff starter, sometimes called firm or dry, produces bread with a more golden crumb and mellower flavor. If you're not baking bread daily or refreshing the starter every day—or if you want a starter that can be stored long term—a stiff starter is preferable to use because it grows more slowly and will collapse more slowly if neglected. A liquid starter, sometimes called wet or sponge, produces bread with a slightly more acidic flavor and slightly larger holes. A stiff starter consists of two-thirds flour to one-third water, while a liquid starter consists of equal weights of flour and water and is refreshed with equal weights of flour and water. All preferments, except wild yeast starters, are made with commercial yeast. You want to be careful that the amount of starter you use is just right; if you use too much, your bread will taste sour and your gluten strands will weaken.

At Orwashers, we use preferments in many of our breads to develop their flavor. Sometimes we use more than one in a recipe. A recipe may call for yeast, which acts as a bit of kick-start to get the fermentation process going. Then we'll also use a biga or other starter to prolong the fermentation process and increase the depth of flavor of the bread. Preferments aren't always necessary, particularly for some of the "simpler" recipes or recipes that call for a lot of flavorful ingredients like cheese or spices, because they do not need the flavor development.

*"Preferments are live, active yeast cultures that are added to the dough to achieve complex flavors and irregular, aerated crumb structures and chewy crusts."*

OPPOSITE PAGE At the early stages of development, carbon dioxide is released and the starter begins to bubble.

# TYPES OF YEAST

There are many different types of yeast available to you for your breads. Some people prefer to use commercial yeast, and others prefer to use wild yeast. Some breads specifically call for wild yeast, like sourdough. Once you have a basic understanding of the different types that exist, you should feel free to experiment with them and see which one you prefer for your breads.

### DRY ACTIVE YEAST

This type of yeast is fresh yeast that has been dehydrated. It comes in the form of granules and is sold in packets or jars. Because it has no moisture, the yeast is considered dormant. In order to make it active, you will need to mix this with some water before mixing it in with your initial ingredients. Even though the yeast is dormant, it still needs to be refrigerated. Make sure to contain it and store it properly to keep it away from moisture and light. This is a common and convenient form of yeast for home bakers.

### RAPID-RISE OR INSTANT YEAST

Rapid-rise or instant yeast is very similar to dry active yeast—but when you use this kind of yeast, the time spent proofing is usually diminished. You also do not need to premix this with water. This type of yeast is used most frequently in our bakery because it does not need to be soaked in order to activate it, which saves a step. It should be kept cool and dry.

### FRESH YEAST

This type of yeast is usually favored by serious bakers. It comes in squares that need to be used very shortly after they are purchased. Since fresh yeast has a large percentage of water in it, the yeast can simply be crumbled in with your other ingredients and mixed. Fresh yeast can be hard to find, and trickier to use than active or instant yeast. Actually, this is my favorite type of yeast to use because I like the way it reacts with bread doughs that require longer fermentation times. We tried using it at Orwashers for a little while, however, but it was not practical in a commercial setting since it requires too much special handling. It can't be exposed to heat before using and it expires quickly. We once lost an entire order (and a day of baking) at the shop because the delivery truck bringing the fresh yeast got stuck in traffic on a hot, sunny day—and by the time it arrived, the entire batch of yeast was unusable. But at home it is easier to control your work conditions, so you may want to try fresh yeast. If you want to substitute fresh yeast for the instant yeast, use three grams of fresh yeast for every one gram of instant yeast called for in the recipe.

### WILD YEAST

Wild yeast is yeast that is grown from scratch, and this is something we do a lot of at Orwashers. After all, this is all bakers could do hundreds of years ago before the invention of commercial yeast. All you need is flour and water to get the yeast growing. Yeast is present in the air we breathe so it is possible to create a starter "out of thin air" with just flour and water and a nice warm environment. We also use grapes, which speeds up the process by infusing the starter with the natural yeast that is also found on the outside of the grapes. There is, of course, a procedure to follow (see Wine Starters, page 108), but the ingredients are simple.

# STIFF STARTERS

## BIGAS

A biga is a preferment used in Italian- and French-style baking. It is typically made from one part water and three parts flour, and some yeast, and has a similar consistency to bread dough. It is useful in breads made from particularly wet doughs because a biga is traditionally the firmest of the preferments; it will therefore add some gluten structure development to a very wet dough. Bigas were created after the invention of commercial yeast, so there was a shift away from wild yeast starter when bigas became available.

## PÂTE FERMENTÉE

This type of stiff starter is French for "old dough." And that's exactly how it is made—by taking a portion of dough from one batch, after it has gone through its first cycle of fermentation, and setting it aside to use later in a different batch of dough as a starter. You can refrigerate this portion of dough for up to two days, or freeze it for up to three months.

# LIQUID STARTERS

## POOLISH

A poolish, sometimes called a sponge, is a preferment used in Italian and French cooking. It is similar to the biga, only a poolish is much more hydrated. Poolishes are typically made from one part flour and one part water, plus a tiny amount of yeast—less yeast than in a biga. A poolish is used to create most of the dough ahead of time, typically ten or twelve hours before the remaining ingredients are mixed in. (This technique was taught to the French by the Polish, hence the name.) You need less yeast in a poolish than a biga because the hydration helps the fermentation along more than a firmer biga would. The higher water content makes it easier for the yeast to convert the sugars into carbon dioxide and alcohol.

## SOURDOUGH LEVAINS, OR WILD STARTERS

A sourdough levain, or wild starter, is a starter that uses wild yeast—not commercial yeast. The term "sourdough" does not necessarily mean these starters are all for sourdough breads. In fact, they can be used in a variety of different types of breads. These starters need to be cared for and refreshed regularly to keep the yeast alive. They are generally made from equal parts of flour and water, but no yeast is added. Instead, the wild yeast is grown by refreshing the mixture with flour and water consistently and regularly. You will need to be patient and wait for the yeast to grow. During the initial stages in the development of a sourdough or levain culture, it is common to add in grapes, water from boiling potatoes, or grated onions. While these can provide an extra nutritional boost and additional flavor, they are not required for success.

Below are the instructions for starters, bigas, and poolishes that you'll need in order to make the bread recipes in the next chapter.

# How to Build the Wine Starter (The Mother)

This recipe will make five pounds of starter. I always feel that larger batches work better and are less susceptible to errors. Also, the starter will have to be strained at the end to remove any grape skins or seeds, so some of it will be lost. The entire process will take five to seven days, depending on conditions.

5-gallon bucket from a home-
  supply store—preferably one
  that comes with a lid (ideally
  a clear plastic container, so
  you can see the process)

I lb/450 g of vineyard grapes,
  destemmed, but not washed

Flour

Water

Day 1

In a deep bowl mix 2.85 lb/1.29 kg cold water and 2.15 lb/ 975.2 g flour by hand. When the mixture is uniform, add the grapes and stir. Cover with lid or super tightly with plastic wrap.

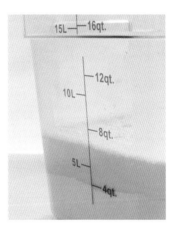 

Day 2

You should see some bleeding of the grapes (the contents will take on a reddish color) and a little activity in the starter in the form of small bubbles.

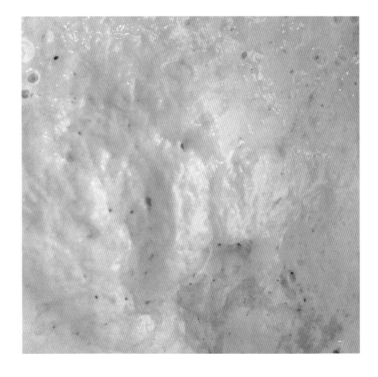

## Day 3

By this time you should see some more air bubbles and the starter should be turning increasingly reddish in color. It might even start to separate a little—don't worry, it's fine! At this point you will need to feed the starter an additional 1.425 lb/646.4 g flour and 1.075 lb/487.6 g cold water and, with your hands, stir or whisk in until smooth. Again, cover tightly.

## Day 4

At this point the fermentation process will be well underway. The starter will be distinctly reddish in color and you will see plenty of bubbles. When you unwrap the bowl, there should be a smell similar to vinegar or the smell coming from an open bottle of wine if if it sits out for a few days.

You will need to reduce the starter by half and add more water and flour. Scoop out half the starter (you can judge it by eye, or do it more precisely by weight), trying to leave as much of the grapes in the bowl as possible. At this point add an additional 1.425 lb/646.4 g flour and 1.075 lb/487.6 g cold water. Stir or whisk in until smooth and then cover tightly.

Day 5

Your starter should really be a bubbling mass of carbon dioxide. This is the home stretch—you are almost there! Make sure you have a larger container handy that will be used to store your starter.

At this point, you need to decide if your starter is active enough to use. How bubbly is it and how does it smell? It should have a stronger smell than on Day 4 and a lot stronger than on Day 3.

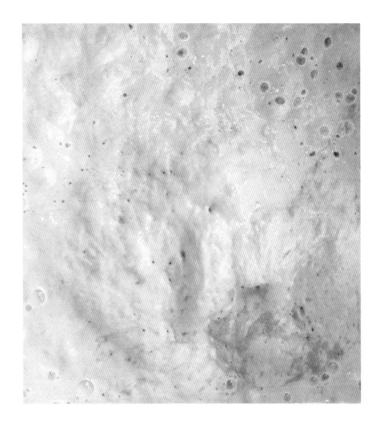

Here are your choices:

A: If you are happy with the results, drain the starter through a strainer into a clean container, removing all the particles of grapes and seeds, and move your starter to the refrigerator for overnight storage. In the morning, you will need to reduce and feed your starter (the same way you did on Day 4) and then allow it to sit for four to six hours before using it.

OR

B: If you feel that your starter could use another day, strain the particles of grapes and seeds, and reduce the starter by half. Add an additional 1.425 lb/646.4 g flour and 1.075 lb/487.6 g cold water and stir or whisk in until smooth. Let sit for four to six hours at room temperature and then refrigerate overnight. Again, allow four to six hours for the starter to come to room temperature before mixing into your first dough.

## HOW TO REFRESH YOUR STARTER:

Once your starter has developed sufficiently, it should be stored in the refrigerator. The mother will last in the refrigerator up to one month. You never want it to get below half of the total amount you started with, however. If you haven't used your preferment for a week or longer, or it's approaching the half level, you will need to refresh in the following manner: Discard half of the starter and add in 1.425 lb/646.4 g flour and 1.075 lb/487.6 g cold water. Stir or whisk in until smooth, and cover tightly. Leave at room temperature for an hour. Then refrigerate overnight and repeat the same process for two or three days, until you are satisfied that it has come back to its previous healthy life of bubbling activity.

You can also freeze your preferment for up to three months. Just thaw it out completely and then follow the refreshing process for three days (or an additional day or two if you are not seeing healthy bubbling activity).

Note: If you ever see a grayish liquid floating on the top of your old starter, skim it off and discard. Do not stir it back into the starter. This will make your starter (and ultimately your breads) much more sour than you would like.

## ADDITIONAL PERFERMENTS

The mother is used to make several of the other preferments you will need to bake the breads in this book. The process for making these starters is similar (although a bit shorter) to the one used for making the mother. Once you've made a batch of the mother, these other preferments will be a natural extension of that process. Find the ingredients on the chart for the starter you want to make, and then follow the instructions below the chart.

ABOVE Whole-wheat biga

RIGHT Dark rye biga

**WHITE RYE BIGA**

| | | |
|---|---|---|
| Rye white flour | 2.90lb/1.32 kg | 100% |
| Water | 1.35 lb/612.3 g | 46 |
| Mother | .75 lb/340.2 g | 25.7 |

**DARK RYE BIGA**

| | | |
|---|---|---|
| Dark rye flour | 1.51 lb/684.9 g | 100% |
| Water | 2 lb/907.2 g | 132 |
| Mother | 1.50 lb/680.4 g | 99 |

**WHITE STARTER**

| | | |
|---|---|---|
| White flour | 1.80 lb/816.5 g | 100% |
| Water | 1.95 lb/884.5 g | 108% |
| Mother | 1.25 lb/567 g | 69% |

**WHOLE-WHEAT BIGA**

| | | |
|---|---|---|
| Whole-wheat flour | 3.05 lb/1.38 kg | 100% |
| Water | 1.93 lb/875.4 g | 63.4 |
| Instant yeast | .01 lb/4.53 g | .3 |

**DURUM BIGA (FOR CIABATTA)**

| | | |
|---|---|---|
| Durum flour | 3.17 lb/ 1.44 kg | 100% |
| Water | 1.82 lb/825.5 g | 57.3 |
| Instant yeast | .003 lb/1.36 g | .09 |

**BAKING TIP:**

Unlike the Mother, these other starters are meant to be made fresh each time you bake. They are not typically stored or refreshed.

1. Mix flour and water together in a deep bowl by hand. Once the mixture is uniform, add the mother or the yeast (depending on what the recipe calls for).

2. Cover tightly and let rest at room temperature (65°F–70°F/18°C–21°C) for 3 to 4 hours.

3. Refrigerate overnight (approximately 12 hours).

4. Leave at room temperature for 3 hours, until there is some activity in the preferment. Make sure it is bubbling (similar to the activity you would see when making a tomato sauce, with a bubble or two popping up every few seconds).

5. Your starter is now ready to use in your recipe.

*Chapter 5*

# THE RECIPES

# BREAD

So now you have been educated on all the basic steps and techniques necessary for artisan bread baking. You've explored quality ingredients and have learned the role of preferments and how to make them. Now, it's finally time to start baking!

The recipes here will provide you with a wide repertoire. The simple, hearty breads and classic rolls are steady staples to accompany everyday meals and provide a palette for all manner of sandwich fillings. The sweeter, specialty breads are more suited for holidays and special occasions.

Remember, like any other craft, bread baking will take time to perfect. It may require baking many loaves to get the excellent taste and texture you desire, and even more experience to be able to reproduce those results consistently. Be prepared to spend time experimenting, and have a curious spirit to explore what does and doesn't work. The troubleshooting guide in Chapter 7 will prove helpful as you examine the fruit of your efforts.

*"The smell of good bread baking,*
*like the sound of lightly flowing water,*
*is indescribable in its evocation of*
*innocence and delight."*

-M. F. K. Fisher

# WHOLE-WHEAT BREAD

If you are looking for something on the hearty side to pair with your morning eggs or afternoon sandwich fixings, you have found it. This whole-wheat bread is simple and slightly sweet with a touch of honey.

Makes 4 loaves.

100%
1179.4 〈 1.3 lbs/589.7 g bread flour

1.3 lbs/589.7 g whole-wheat flour

50%  1.3 lbs/589.7 g water

5.7  .15 lb/68.04 g honey

5.7  .15 lb/68.04 g vegetable oil

26.14  .68 lb/308.4 g white starter
        (see page 113)

2.3  .06 lb/27.22 g salt

1.9  .05 lb/22.68 g sugar

.38.  .01 lb/4.54 g instant yeast

1. Set up stand mixer with a dough hook.

2. Place both flours, water, honey, oil, white starter, salt, sugar, and yeast in mixing bowl.

3. Mix on medium-low for 4 minutes.

4. Mix on medium-high for 8 minutes.

5. Dough temperature should be between 76°F and 78°F/24°C and 26°C.

6. Dough should appear shiny and pull away from the mixing bowl.

7. Do the dough test (see page 47).

8. Take dough out of mixing bowl and transfer to lightly oiled airtight container.

9. Let dough rest on countertop for approximately 1 hour and 45 minutes. Dough should double in size.

10. Roll dough out of container onto a lightly floured work surface (marble or butcher block is ideal).

11. Cut dough with a scraper into 4 even squares/rectangles, approximately 1.25 lbs/567 g each.

12. Shape each into a boule (see page 64).

13. Let dough rest 3 hours after shaping.

14. Score an "X" into the top of the dough before baking.

15. Preheat oven to 410°F/210°C.

16. Bake for 40 minutes until the crust is golden.

# MULTIGRAIN BREAD

A light and airy whole-wheat dough sprinkled with millet, coarse rye, oats, and sunflower and flax seeds—add some crunch to your lunchtime sandwich.

Makes 4 loaves.

1.63 lbs/739.4 g bread flour ⎤ 100% 1057

.7 lb/317.5 g whole-wheat flour ⎦

1.33 lbs/603.3 g water 57%

.23 lb/104.3 g honey 9.8%

.15 lb/68.04 g dark rye starter 6.43%
  (see page 113)

.5 lb/226.8 g white starter 21.45%
  (see page 113)

.06 lb/27.22 g salt 2.57

.4 lb/181.4 g grain mix 17.16 — 3.43 of each
  (see box)

.01 lb/4.54 g instant yeast .42%

1. Set up stand mixer with a dough hook.

2. Place both types of flour, water, honey, dark rye starter, white starter, salt, grain mix, and yeast in mixing bowl.

3. Mix on medium-low for 4 minutes.

4. Mix on medium-high for 8 minutes.

5. Dough temperature should be between 76°F and 78°F/24°C and 26°C.

6. Dough should appear shiny and pull away from the mixing bowl.

7. Do the dough test (see page 47).

8. Take dough out of mixing bowl and transfer to lightly oiled airtight container.

9. Let dough rest on countertop for approximately 1 hour and 45 minutes. Dough should double in size.

10. Roll dough out of container onto a lightly floured work surface (marble or butcher block is ideal).

11. Cut dough with a scraper into 4 even squares/rectangles, approximately 1.25 lbs/567 g each.

12. Shape each into a free-form oval (see page 61) and cover.

13. Let dough rest 3 hours after shaping.

14. Preheat oven to 450°F/225°C.

15. Bake for 40 minutes until crust is golden.

The grain mix is what gives this bread its complex and hearty character. Orwashers uses equal parts of the following grains and seeds: millet, coarse rye, oats, and sunflower and flax seeds, but you can experiment and substitute other grains or seeds to your liking.

# WHITE BREAD

Nothing beats a classic white bread for lunchtime sandwiches. This traditional take on a white bread will bring you back to your peanut butter and jelly brown bag lunches of yesterday.

Makes 4 loaves.

2.95 lbs/1.34 kg bread flour *100%*

1.62 lbs/734.82 water *55%*

.23 lb/104.3 g sugar *7.0% ?*

.13 lb/58.97 g vegetable oil *4.0%*

.06 lb/27.22 g salt *2%*

.03 lb/13.61 g instant yeast *1%*

1.  Set up stand mixer with a dough hook.

2.  Place flour, sugar, oil, salt, and yeast in mixing bowl.

3.  Mix on medium-low for 4 minutes.

4.  Mix on medium-high for 8 minutes.

5.  Dough temperature should be between 76°F and 78°F/24°C and 26°C.

6.  Dough should appear shiny and pull away from the mixing bowl.

7.  Do the dough test (see page 47).

8.  Take dough out of mixing bowl and transfer to lightly oiled airtight container.

9.  Let dough rest on countertop for approximately 30 minutes. Dough should double in size.

10. Roll dough out of container onto a lightly floured work surface (marble or butcher block is ideal).

11. Cut dough with a scraper into 4 even squares/rectangles, approximately 1.25 lbs/567 g each.

12. Shape each into a boule (see page 60), or a Pullman loaf placed into a pan (see page 64).

13. If shaping into a boule, score an "X" in the top. If the loaf is in a Pullman pan, score 3 diagonal cuts across the top, about 1.5 in/3.75 cm apart.

14. Let dough rest 4 hours after shaping.

15. Preheat oven to 400°F/205°C.

16. Bake for 40 minutes until crust is golden.

# New York Rye Bread

Rye bread is a New York institution. Our recipe for rye bread is the definition of old-world flavor. It has been a metropolitan favorite through the generations because of its chewy and sour interior generously decorated with caraway seeds, and a chewy crust. Rye bread is the ultimate pairing for cured meats and cheeses and just the right loaf for a truly New York deli sandwich.

Makes 4 loaves.

2.44 lbs/1.11 kg *100%* bread flour

1 lb/453.6 g rye biga *40%* (see page 113)

1.4 1lbs/639.6 g water *57%*

.09 lb/40.82 g salt *3.6%*

.02 lb/9.07 g *.8%* instant yeast

.1 lb/45.36 g caraway *4%* seeds (optional)

1. Set up stand mixer with a dough hook.
2. Place flour, rye biga, water, salt, yeast, and caraway seeds in mixing bowl.
3. Mix on medium-low for 4 minutes.
4. Mix on medium-high for 7 minutes.
5. Dough temperature should be between 76°F and 78°F/24°C and 26°C.
6. Dough should appear shiny and pull away from the mixing bowl.
7. Do the dough test (see page 47).
8. Take dough out of mixing bowl and transfer to lightly oiled airtight container.
9. Let dough rest on countertop for approximately 2 hours. Dough should double in size.
10. Roll dough out of container onto a lightly floured work surface (marble or butcher block is ideal).
11. Cut dough with a scraper into 4 even squares/rectangles, approximately 1.25 lbs/567 g each.
12. Shape each into a free-form oval (see page 61).
13. After shaping, cover the dough with plastic wrap and let it rest 6 hours in the refrigerator.
14. Then let it sit out on the counter for 90 minutes.
15. Make 4-5 scores in the dough across the shorter width of the loaf. Scores should be 1 in/2.5 cm apart and approximately 1 in/2.5 cm from either end of the dough.
16. Preheat oven to 475°F/245°C.
17. Bake for 40 minutes until crust is golden.

# Pumpernickel Bread

---

Inspired by traditional Eastern European breads, this dark rye is sweetened with a deep-amber-colored molasses. The subtle sweetness carried by these loaves is complemented by the tangy rye undertones.

Makes 4 loaves.

2.47 lbs/1.12 kg bread flour

.51 lb/231.3 g rye biga (see page 113)

1.54 lbs/244.94 g water

.08 lb/36.29 g molasses

.11 lb/49.9 g brewed coffee, at room temperature

.07 lb/313.75 g salt

.02 lb/9.07 g instant yeast

.2 lb/90.72 g raisins (optional. The juicier the better; dry raisins will not yield the ideal result.)

.2 lb/90.72 g walnut halves or pieces of walnuts, not crushed (optional)

1. Set up stand mixer with a dough hook.
2. Place flour, rye biga, water, molasses, coffee, salt, and yeast in mixing bowl.
3. Mix on medium-low for 4 minutes.
4. Mix on medium-high for 7 minutes if using raisins and walnuts, mix for only 6 minutes; add raisins and walnuts and then mix for 2 more minutes.
5. Dough temperature should be between 76°F and 78°F/24°C and 26°C.
6. Dough should appear shiny and pull away from the mixing bowl.
7. Do the dough test, (see page 47).
8. Take dough out of mixing bowl and transfer to lightly oiled airtight container.
9. Let dough rest on countertop for approximately 1 hour and 30 minutes. Dough should double in size.
10. Roll dough out of container onto a lightly floured work surface (marble or butcher block is ideal).
11. Cut dough with a scraper into 4 even squares/rectangles, approximately 1.25 lbs/567 g each.
12. Shape each into a free-form oval (see page 61). We like to make the raisin walnut pumpernickel in a loaf pan at the bakery. Feel free to try this variation as well. If you are adding walnuts, sprinkle a few additional walnuts at the bottom of your loaf pan and place the dough on top of them.
13. Let dough rest 4 hours after shaping.
14. Make 4-5 scores in the dough across the shorter width of the loaf. Scores should be 1 in/2.5 cm apart and approximately 1 in/2.5 cm from either end of the dough.
15. Preheat oven to 440°F/230°C.
16. Bake for 35 minutes until crust is dark brown.

# MARBLE RYE

Marble rye is a delicious bread that is great for both toast and sandwiches. Marble rye is a mix of the two most famous New York breads, plain rye and pumpernickel. The "marble" aspect to the name of this bread comes from the technique of shaping the rye and pumpernickel doughs into one.

Makes 4 loaves.

For Rye Dough:

1.25 lbs/567 g bread flour

.5 lb/226.79 g rye biga
(see page 113)

.71 lb/322.05 g water

.04 lb/18.14 g salt

.01 lb/4.53 g instant yeast

For Pumpernickel Dough:

1.25 lbs/567 g bread flour

.25 lb/113.39 g rye biga
(see page 113)

.76 lb/344.73 g water

.04 lb/18.14 g molasses

.06 lb/27.21 g brewed coffee,
at room temperature

.03 lb/13.60 g salt

.008 lb/3.62 g instant yeast

Using the proportions of ingredients on the left, follow the instructions for making rye and pumpernickel breads (see pages 124 and 127), until the shaping step. The technique for shaping marble rye is as follows:

1.  Take each dough from its resting bucket and place on your work surface.
2.  Use your fingertips to gently push out each dough into a rectangle shape, roughly 8 in/20 cm by 6 in/15 cm.
3.  Then place the rye dough on top of the pumpernickel dough.
4.  Fold the dough in half.
5.  Cut with a scraper into 4 even squares/rectangles, approximately 1.25 lbs/567 g each.
6.  Shape each into a free-form oval (see page 61). You can also shape this bread into a Pullman loaf.
7.  Preheat oven to 440°F/230°C.
8.  Bake for 35 minutes or until rye portion is golden.

# Soho Sourdough Bread

Our Soho sourdough takes almost 36 hours to create, and it challenges the tang of its West Coast rivals. Our robust wine starter lends itself to a mature sour flavor and aroma. A thick slice and chewy crust provide the base for an awesome grilled cheese sandwich.

Makes 4 loaves.

2.63 lbs/1.19 kg
bread flour
.08 lb/36.29 g whole-
wheat flour

*100%*
*1226.29*

1.2 lbs/544.3 g water *44.59%*

1 lb/453.6 g
white starter
(see page 113) *37%*

.08 lb/36.29 g salt *2.96*

.002 lb/.98 g
instant yeast *0.08%*

1. Set up stand mixer with a dough hook.
2. Place bread flour, whole-wheat flour, water, white starter, salt, and yeast in mixing bowl.
3. Mix on medium-low for 4 minutes.
4. Mix on medium-high for 8 minutes.
5. Dough temperature should be between 76°F and 78°F/24°C and 26°C.
6. Dough should appear shiny and pull away from the mixing bowl.
7. Do the dough test (see page 47).
8. Take dough out of mixing bowl and transfer to lightly oiled airtight container.
9. Let dough rest on countertop for approximately 4 hours. Dough should double in size.
10. Roll dough out of container onto a lightly floured work surface (marble or butcher block is ideal).
11. Cut dough with a scraper into 4 even squares/rectangles, approximately 1.25 lbs/567 g each.
12. Shape each into a boule (see page 60).
13. After shaping, let dough rest for a minimum of 24 hours and up to 30 hours in your refrigerator. Make sure to wrap the dough with plastic wrap so it doesn't dry out and form a skin.
14. Remove boules from refrigerator and let rest on your kitchen counter uncovered until fully proofed. That can take from 2 to 3 hours, depending on the temperature and humidity in the kitchen.
15. Score an "X" on the top of the dough.
16. Preheat oven to 475°F/245°C.
17. Bake for 50 minutes until bread is lightly golden.

# CIABATTA BREAD

Taking influence from the Liguria region of Italy, our rustic ciabatta is light and aromatic. Just waiting to be toasted, this is the perfect loaf for sandwiches, bruschetta, and dipping in olive oil.

Makes 4 loaves.

2.3 lbs/1.04 kg bread flour  *100%*

1.73 lbs/784.7 g water  *75%*

.1 lb/45.36 g olive oil  *~~%~~ 4.36b*

.75 lb/340.2 g biga  *32%*
  (see page 113)

.07 lb/31.75 g salt  *3.0%*

.02 lb/9.07 g instant yeast  *.87%*

1. Set up stand mixer with a dough hook.
2. Place flour and water in mixing bowl.
3. Mix on low until combined.
4. Cover bowl with a damp cloth, or towel, and let rest for 10 minutes.
5. Add oil, biga, salt, and yeast to mixing bowl.
6. Mix on medium-low for 4 minutes.
7. Mix on medium-high for 8 minutes.
8. Dough temperature should be between 72°F and 74°F/22°C and 23°C.
9. Dough should appear shiny and pull away from the mixing bowl.
10. Do the dough test (see page 47).
11. Take dough out of mixing bowl and transfer to lightly oiled airtight container.
12. Let dough rest on countertop for approximately 1 hour and 30 minutes. Dough should double in size.
13. Roll dough out of container onto a lightly floured work surface (marble or butcher block is ideal).
14. Shape, using the ciabatta shaping technique (see page 63).
16. Let dough proof for 1 hour.
17. Preheat oven to 415°F/215°C.
18. Bake for 25 minutes until bread is golden.

# OLIVE BREAD

This olive bread is a fantastic way to "wow" your dinner guests with something that is different from your average table bread. The addition of olives gives the dough the perfect amount of saltiness.

Makes 4 loaves.

1.73 lbs/784.7 g bread flour       *100%*

.5 lb/226.8 g whole-wheat flour    *1011*

1.39 lbs/630.5 g water    *62.36%*

.45 lb/204.1 g white starter    *20.18%*
   (see page 113)

.06 lb/27.22 g olive oil    *2.7%*

.05 lb/22.68 g salt    *2.24%*

.01 lb/4.54 g thyme    *.44%*

.02 lb/9.07 g instant yeast    *.89%*

.8 lb/362.0 g olives    *35%*
   (I suggest pitted black
   and green olive pieces)

1. Set up stand mixer with a dough hook.
2. Place bread flour, whole-wheat flour, water, white starter, oil, salt, thyme, and yeast in mixing bowl.
3. Mix on medium-low for 4 minutes.
4. Mix on medium-high for 7 minutes.
5. Add olives.
6. Mix on low for 2 minutes.
7. Dough temperature should be between 72°F and 74°F/22°C and 23°C.
8. Dough should appear shiny and pull away from the mixing bowl.
9. Do the dough test (see page 47).
10. Take dough out of mixing bowl and transfer to lightly oiled airtight container.
11. Let dough rest in container for 1 hour.
12. Fold (see page 59) and put back in container.
13. Let dough rest on countertop for approximately 3 hours. Dough should double in size.
14. Roll dough out of container onto a lightly floured work surface (marble or butcher block is ideal).
15. Cut dough with a scraper into 4 even squares/rectangles, approximately 1.25 lbs/567 g each.
16. Shape each into a rustic free-form (see page 65).
17. Let dough rest 3 hours after shaping.
18. Score one long cut along the length of the loaf.
19. Preheat oven to 475°F/245°C.
20. Bake for 45 minutes until crust is dark and well baked.

# FOCACCIA

This pizza-like bread is light and airy and a great base recipe for those bakers who are looking to experiment with different add-ins (think of onion, garlic, olives, and so on). This basic recipe results in a bread that's great for accompanying a meal or toasting up to make a panini.

Makes 2 loaves.

2.50 lbs/1.14 kg bread flour    *100%*

1.51 lbs/689.4 g water    *60%*

.1 lb/45.26 g olive oil    *4%*

.78 lb/353.8 g white starter    *31%*
   (see page 113)

.07 lb/31.75 g salt    *2.78*

.04 lb/18.14 g sugar    *1.59.*

.01 lb/4.54 g instant yeast    *.39.*

1. Set up stand mixer with a dough hook.
2. Place flour and water in mixing bowl.
3. Mix on low until combined.
4. Cover bowl with a damp cloth, or towel, and let rest for 10 minutes.
5. Add oil, white starter, salt, sugar, and yeast to mixing bowl.
6. Mix on medium-low for 4 minutes.
7. Mix on medium-high for 8 minutes.
8. Dough temperature should be between 72°F and 74°F/22°C and 23°C.
9. Dough should appear shiny and pull away from the mixing bowl.
10. Do the dough test (see page 47).
11. Take dough out of mixing bowl and transfer to lightly oiled airtight container.
12. Let dough rest on countertop for approximately 4 hours. Dough should double in size.
13. Roll dough out of container onto a lightly floured work surface (marble or butcher block is ideal).
14. Divide dough in half, approximately 2.5 lbs/1.134 kg per piece.
15. Fold each piece in half. Allow dough to rest for 2 hours.
16. Shape each piece, using the focaccia shaping technique (see page 62).
17. Let dough proof for one and a half hours after pressing into trays.
18. Before baking, spray or gently brush with your favorite olive oil. You can use an oil infused with a flavor—for example, herb, chili, or garlic—to get a different taste.
19. Preheat oven to 420°F/215°C.
20. Bake for 25 minutes until golden.

# RUSSIAN BREAD

Similar to the pumpernickel bread, this recipe includes rye grain for a slightly more sour tang.

Makes 4 loaves.

2.49 lbs/1.13 kg bread flour

.5 lb/226.8 g rye biga
(see page 113)

1.53 lbs/694 g water

.23 lb/104.3 g rye flakes

.07 lb/31.75 g molasses

.11 lb/49.9 g caramel color

.06 lb/27.22 g salt

.02 lb/9.07 g instant yeast

1.  Set up stand mixer with a dough hook.

2.  Place flour, rye biga, water, rye flakes, molasses, caramel color, salt, and yeast in mixing bowl

3.  Mix on medium-low for 4 minutes.

4.  Mix on medium-high for 8 minutes.

5.  Dough temperature should be between 76°F and 78°F/24°C and 26°C.

6.  Dough should appear shiny and pull away from the mixing bowl.

7.  Do the dough test (see page 47).

8.  Take dough out of mixing bowl and transfer to lightly oiled airtight container.

9.  Let dough rest on countertop for approximately 1 hour and 30 minutes. Dough should double in size.

10. Roll dough out of container onto a lightly floured work surface (marble or butcher block is ideal).

11. Cut dough with a scraper into 4 even squares/rectangles, approximately 1.25 lbs/567 g each.

12. Shape each into a free-form oval (see page 61).

13. Let dough rest 4 hours after shaping.

14. Make 4-5 scores in the dough across the shorter width of the loaf. Scores should be 1 in/2.5 cm apart and approximately 1 in/2.5 cm from either end of the dough.

15. Preheat oven to 410°F/210°C.

16. Bake for 45 minutes until crust is dark brown.

# Challah Bread

This egg bread is light and slightly sweet, making it perfect for French toast, bread puddings, stuffing, or croutons. Go ahead and experiment with mix-ins as well. This recipe would also be great with the addition of some dried fruit or nuts (or both).

Makes 4 loaves.

2.77 lbs/1.26 kg *100%* bread flour

1.25 lbs/567 g water *45%*

.4 lb/181.4 g *14.39%* egg yolks

.2 lb/90.72 g vegetable *72%* shortening

.31 lb/140.6 g sugar *11.15%*

.05 lb/ 22.67 g salt *1.79%*

.03 lb/13.61 g *1.08%* instant yeast

1. Set up stand mixer with a dough hook.
2. Place flour, water, egg yolks, shortening, sugar, and salt in mixing bowl.
3. Mix on medium-low for 5 minutes.
4. Mix on medium-high for 2 minutes.
5. Add yeast.
6. Mix on medium for an additional 6 minutes.
7. Dough temperature should be between 76°F and 78°F/ 24°C and 26°C.
8. Dough should appear shiny and pull away from the mixing bowl.
9. Do the dough test (see page 47).
10. Take dough out of mixing bowl and transfer to a lightly oiled airtight container.
11. Let dough rest on countertop for approximately 3 hours. Dough should double in size.
12. Roll dough out of container onto a lightly floured work surface (marble or butcher block is ideal).
13. Cut dough with a scraper into 4 even squares/rectangles, approximately 1.25 lbs/567 g each.
14. Shape each into a braided loaf (see page 66). This bread is traditionally braided—but if you are having a difficult time learning how to braid dough, the bread can be shaped as a loaf and baked in your bread pan. It will taste just as good!
15. Let dough rest 2 hours after shaping.
16. Preheat oven to 400°F/205°C.
17. Bake for 10 minutes.
18. Change the oven temperature to 330°F/160°C and bake until golden brown, approximately an additional 30 minutes.

# Holiday Challah Bread

Now a holiday favorite, I created Holiday Challah as a sweet and light-hearted way to celebrate seasonal festivities. This bread has a beautiful interior that is sprinkled with color from the dried fruit and pistachios. The Holiday Challah is great as toast with tea or coffee—or even better, slice it thinly and bake the slices on a sheet pan until crisp, making a biscotti-like treat.

Makes 4 loaves.

| | |
|---|---|
| 1.9 lbs/861.8 g bread flour | 1. Set up stand mixer with a dough hook. |
| 1.2 lbs/544.3 g water | 2. Place flour, water, egg yolks, oil, sugar, and salt in mixing bowl. |
| .25 lb/113.4 g egg yolks | 3. Mix on medium-low for 5 minutes. |
| .1 lb/45.36 g vegetable oil | 4. Mix on medium-high for 2 minutes. |
| | 5. Add yeast. |
| .05 lb/22.68 g sugar | 6. Mix on medium for an additional 6 minutes. |
| .04 lb/18.14 g salt | 7. Add cranberries, golden raisins, pistachios, and orange zest. |
| .03 lb/13.61 g instant yeast | 8. Mix on low until dry ingredients are combined into dough. |
| .4 lb/181.4 g cranberries | 9. Dough temperature should be between 76°F and 78°F/24°C and 26°C. |
| .5 lb/226.8 g golden raisins | 10. Dough should appear shiny and pull away from the mixing bowl |
| .35 lb/158.8 pistachios | 11. Do the dough test (see page 47). |
| .18 lb/81.65 g orange zest | 12. Take dough out of mixing bowl and transfer to lightly oiled airtight container. |

13. Let dough rest on counter top for approximately 3 hours. Dough should double in size.

14. Roll dough out of container onto a lightly floured work surface (marble or butcher block is ideal).

15. Cut dough with a scraper into 4 even squares/rectangles, approximately 1.25 lbs/567 g each.

16. Shape each into a boule (see page 60).

17. Let dough rest 4 hours after shaping.

18. Score an "X" in the top of the loaf.

19. Preheat oven to 390°F/200°C.

20. Bake for 33 minutes until lightly golden brown.

# Cinnamon Raisin Bread

Our cinnamon raisin breads have sweetened weekend breakfasts for nearly one hundred years, and are the ultimate Sunday morning ritual. Bursting with cinnamon and sugar, it brings French toast to a new level.

Makes 4 loaves.

2.52 lbs/1.14 kg bread flour

1.49 lbs/675.9 g water

.08 lb/36.29 g vegetable oil

.1 lb/45.46 g sugar

.05 lb/22.68 g salt

.03 lb/13.61 g instant yeast

.7 lb/31.75 g raisins

Cinnamon Sugar Mix:

.01 lb/4.55 g cinnamon

.05 lb/22.68 g sugar

.05 lb/22.68 g vegetable shortening

.7 lb/31.75 g walnut halves or pieces, not crushed (optional)

1. Set up stand mixer with a dough hook.
2. Place flour, water, oil, sugar, salt, and yeast in mixing bowl.
3. Mix on medium-low for 4 minutes. Then mix on medium-high for 6 minutes.
4. Add raisins and mix on low for 1 minute.
5. Dough temperature should be between 76°F and 78°F/24°C and 26°C.
6. Dough should appear shiny and pull away from the mixing bowl.
9. Do the dough test (see page 47).
7. Transfer to a lightly oiled airtight container.
8. Let dough rest on countertop for approximately 30 minutes. Dough should double in size.
9. Roll dough out of container onto a lightly floured work surface (marble or butcher block is ideal).
10. Cut dough with a scraper into 4 even squares/rectangles, approximately 1.25 lbs/567 g each.
11. Flatten out dough into a rectangle shape by gently pushing it down with your fingertips. Then evenly and generously spread approximately one quarter of your cinnamon sugar mix on top of the dough (similar to the way you spread peanut butter on a slice of bread). Fold dough in half.
12. Shape into a boule (see page 60) or a Pullman loaf (see page 64). Place in loaf pans. (At the bakery we shape the cinnamon raisin in a boule and the cinnamon raisin with walnuts into a pan loaf. If using walnuts, sprinkle a few additional nuts in the bottom of your pan loaf before adding the dough.)
13. Let dough rest 4 hours after shaping. (This bread is not scored.)
14. Preheat oven to 400°F/205°C.
15. Bake for 13 minutes and adjust oven temperature to 380°F/190°C.
16. Bake an additional 4 minutes until bread is golden.

# Pumpkin Bread

This seasonal bread has a cult following at the bakery, with customers begging us to keep it around beyond pumpkin season and pleading for its return in early autumn. My pumpkin bread recipe is slightly sweet and much lighter than your traditional pumpkin quick bread. It is perfect as toast with a dab of butter, but makes phenomenal French toast, bread pudding, or the ultimate fall-inspired stuffing.

Makes 4 loaves.

2.45 lbs/1.11 kg bread flour

.49 lb/222.3 g water

.93 lb/421.8 g pure pumpkin

.01 lb/4.54 g cinnamon

.01 lb/4.54 g nutmeg

.01 lb/4.54 g mace

.01 lb/4.55 g ginger

.25 lb/113.4 g eggs

.25 lb/113.4 g vegetable oil

.1 lb/45.36 g malt

.43 lb/195 g sugar

.05 lb/22.68 g salt

.02 lb/9.07 instant yeast

1. Set up stand mixer with a dough hook.
2. Place bread flour, water, pumpkin, cinnamon, nutmeg, mace, ginger, eggs, oil, malt, sugar, salt, and yeast in mixing bowl.
3. Mix on medium-low for 5 minutes.
4. Mix on medium-high for 10 minutes.
5. Dough temperature should be between 76°F and 78°F/ 24°C and 26°C.
6. Dough should appear shiny and pull away from the mixing bowl.
7. Do the dough test (see page 47).
8. Take dough out of mixing bowl and transfer to lightly oiled airtight container.
9. Let dough rest on countertop for approximately 3 hours. Dough should double in size.
10. Roll dough roll out of container onto a lightly floured work surface (marble or butcher block is ideal).
11. Cut dough with a scraper into 4 even squares/rectangles, approximately 1.25 lbs/567 g each.
12. Shape each into a boule (see page 60).
13. Let dough rest 4 hours after shaping.
14. Score an "X" into the top of the dough before baking.
15. Preheat oven to 400°F/205°C.
16. Bake for 5 minutes, and then change the oven temperature to 340°F/170°C.
17. Bake for an additional 25 minutes until golden brown.

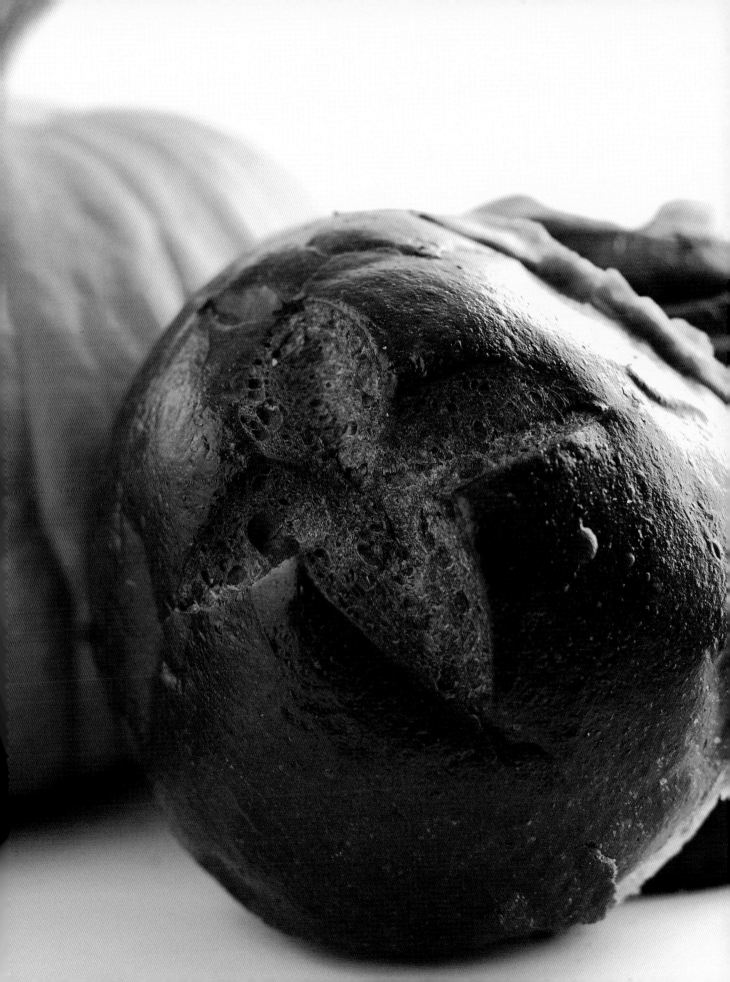

# CHOCOLATE BREAD

This recipe is a challah-based bread that is studded with chocolate chips. We bake it around Valentine's Day at the bakery, but it is perfect for any sweet occasion! Chocolate bread makes for a decadent breakfast or a sweet snack.

Makes 4 loaves.

2.46 lbs/1.12 kg bread flour

1.25 lbs/567 g water

.1 lb/45.36 g egg yolks

.2 lb/90.72 g solid vegetable shortening

.4 lb/181.4 g sugar

.01 lb/4.54 g cinnamon

.05 lb/22.68 g salt

.03 lb/13.61 g instant yeast

.5 lb/226.8 g chocolate chunks (I like to use semi-sweet chocolate, but any will do; it's really a matter of preference. However, I feel dark chocolate with a high cocoa content is too bitter for this bread.)

1. Set up stand mixer with a dough hook.
2. Place flour, water, egg yolks, vegetable shortening, sugar, cinnamon, and salt in mixing bowl.
3. Mix on medium-low for 5 minutes.
4. Mix on medium-high for 2 minutes.
5. Add yeast.
6. Mix on medium for an additional 6 minutes.
7. Add chocolate chunks.
8. Mix on low until chocolate is combined in dough.
9. Dough temperature should be between 76°F and 78°F/ 24°C and 26°C.
10. Dough should appear shiny and pull away from the mixing bowl
11. Do the dough test (see page 47).
12. Take dough out of mixing bowl and transfer to lightly oiled airtight container.
13. Let dough rest on countertop for approximately 3 hours. Dough should double in size.
14. Let dough roll out of container onto a lightly floured work surface (marble or butcher block is ideal).
15. Cut dough with a scraper into 4 even squares/rectangles, approximately 1.25 lbs/567 g each.
16. Shape each into a boule (see page 60).
17. Let dough rest 4 hours after shaping.
18. Score an "X" into the top of the dough. (We like to score a heart into the top of this bread for Valentine's Day. Try making a small heart shape on top of the bread instead of an "X.")
19. Preheat oven to 390°F/200°C.
20. Bake for 33 minutes until lightly golden brown.

# Irish Soda Bread

This spin on Irish soda bread is lighter than the original. The customers at the bakery love the way it toasts up perfectly, and it's even better when spread with a generous pat of European butter.

Makes 4 loaves.

2.45 lbs/1.11 kg bread flour

1.50 lbs/680.34 g water

.08 lb/36.29 g vegetable oil

.1 lb/45.36 g sugar

.05 lb/22.68 g salt

.03 lb/13.61 g instant yeast

.7 lb/317.5 g raisins

.1 lb/45.36 g caraway seeds (optional)

1. Set up stand mixer with a dough hook.
2. Place flour, water, oil, sugar, salt, and yeast in mixing bowl.
3. Mix on medium-low for 4 minutes.
4. Mix on medium-high for 6 minutes.
5. Add raisins and caraway seeds.
6. Mix on low for 1 minute.
7. Dough temperature should be between 76°F and 78°F/24°C and 26°C.
8. Dough should appear shiny and pull away from the mixing bowl.
9. Do the dough test (see page 47).
10. Take dough out of mixing bowl and transfer to lightly oiled airtight container.
11. Let dough rest on countertop for approximately 30 minutes. Dough should double in size.
12. Roll dough out of container onto a lightly floured work surface (marble or butcher block is ideal).
13. Cut dough with a scraper into 4 even squares/rectangles, approximately 1.25 lbs/567 g each.
14. Shape each into a boule (see page 60).
15. Let dough rest 4 hours after shaping.
16. Score an "X" into the top of the dough.
17. Preheat oven to 410°F/210°C.
18. Bake for 18 minutes until bread is lightly golden.

# Fruit Focaccia

*This spin on focaccia, a pizza-like bread, brings what is typically a savory bread into the land of the sweet. This is perfect to bake around the holidays or when celebrating a special occasion. Serve at breakfast or dessert.*

Makes 2 loaves.

1.9 lbs/861.8 g bread flour

1.4 lbs/635 g water

.13 lb/58.97 g vegetable
　　shortening

.76 lb/344.7 g white starter
　　(see page 113)

.05 lb/22.68 g salt

.25 lb/113.4 g sugar

.635 lb/288 g golden raisins

.625 lb/283.5 g cranberries

.018 lb/8.17 g instant yeast

Turbinado sugar for sprinkling

1. Set up stand mixer with a dough hook.
2. Place flour, water, vegetable shortening, salt, sugar, and yeast in mixing bowl.
3. Mix on medium-low for 4 minutes.
4. Mix on medium-high for 8 minutes.
5. Add golden raisins and cranberries. Mix on low until combined.
6. Dough temperature should be between 76°F and 78°F/ 24°C and 26°C.
7. Dough should appear shiny and pull away from the mixing bowl.
8. Do the dough test (see page 47).
9. Take dough out of mixing bowl and transfer to lightly oiled airtight container.
10. Let dough rest on countertop for approximately 4 hours. Dough should double in size.
11. Roll dough roll out of container onto a lightly floured work surface (marble or butcher block is ideal).
12. Divide dough in half, approximately 2.5 lbs/1.13 kg per piece.
13. Fold each piece in half. Allow dough to rest for 2 hours.
14. Shape, using the focaccia technique (see page 62).
15. Once shaped, cover with plastic wrap and refrigerate overnight, approximately 12 hours.
16. Let rest at room temperature for an hour.
17. Sprinkle generously with turbinado sugar before putting in the oven.
18. Preheat oven to 420°F/215°C.
19. Bake for 25 minutes until lightly golden brown.

# BUNS

There is a renewed passion for making really good burgers. Going beyond chuck or sirloin, restaurants are using very rich blends of meat and so require a bun that is light and fluffy, with a delicate crust and just the right bit of resistance. Now you can re-create that restaurant style burger, bun included, in your own home. The nice thing here is that all your hard work won't go to waste. Wrapped tightly in a freezer bag, these will last for three to four weeks in the freezer.

# Burger Buns

The challenge with burger buns is creating a bun that accompanies the burger in a way that doesn't overpower the meat and the toppings. These burger buns are light and airy, but have just enough substance to stand up to your most adventurous accompaniment.

Makes approximately 22 burger buns.

2.85 lbs/1.29 g bread flour

1.46 lbs/662.24 g water

.21 lb/95.25 g vegetable oil

.06 lb/27.21 g salt

.08 lb/36.28 g malt

.35 lb/158.75 g sugar

.05 lb/22.67 g instant yeast

1. Set up stand mixer with a dough hook.
2. Place flour, water, oil, salt, and malt in mixing bowl.
3. Mix on medium-low for 3 minutes.
4. Add sugar and yeast.
5. Mix on medium-low for 1 additional minute.
6. Mix on medium-high for 8 minutes.
7. Dough temperature should be between 76°F and 78°F/24°C and 26°C.
8. Dough should appear shiny and pull away from the mixing bowl.
9. Do the dough test (see page 47).
10. Turn dough out of mixing bowl onto a lightly floured work surface (marble or butcher block is ideal).
11. Cut dough with a scraper into 3.5-oz/99.22-g pieces.
12. Shape like dinner rolls (see page 68).
13. Place on a parchment-lined sheet tray, approximately 2 in/5cm apart.
14. Let dough rest 4 hours after shaping.
15. Preheat oven to 400°F/205°C.
16. Bake for 16 minutes until lightly golden brown.

# Potato Burger Buns

The addition of potato flour to this burger bun recipe makes these buns slightly more soft and doughy. Though a subtle difference, it's one that elevates your burger to the next level. Feel free to add sesame seeds to the top before baking for an added crunch.

Makes approximately 22 burger buns.

2.8 lbs/1.27 kg bread flour

1.56 lbs/707.60 g water

.21 lb/95.25 g vegetable oil

.26 lb/117.93 g sugar

.06 lb/27.21 g salt

.17 lb/77.11 g potato flour

.04 lb/18.14 g instant yeast

1. Set up stand mixer with a dough hook.
2. Place spring flour, water, oil, sugar, and salt in mixing bowl.
3. Mix on medium-low for 3 minutes.
4. Add potato flour and yeast.
5. Mix on medium-low for an additional 1 minute.
6. Mix on high for an additional 8 minutes.
7. Dough temperature should be between 76°F and 78°F/24°C and 26°C.
8. Dough should appear shiny and pull away from the mixing bowl.
9. Do the dough test (see page 47).
10. Take dough out of mixing bowl onto a lightly floured work surface (marble or butcher block is ideal).
11. Cut dough with a scraper and chunk into 3.5-oz/99.22-g pieces.
12. Shape like dinner rolls (see page 68).
13. Place on a parchment-lined sheet tray, approximately 2 in/5 cm.
14. Let dough rest 4 hours after shaping.
15. Preheat oven to 400°F/205°C.
16. Bake for 16 minutes until lightly golden brown.

# ROLLS

While our buns are recipes unto themselves, for many of our other rolls we use the same delicious doughs that we use to make breads—but just shape them differently.

# ONION POCKETS

These are a longtime favorite of our customers and a real embodiment of NYC-style bread.

Makes approximately 26 rolls.

1. Make one recipe for white bread dough (see page 122).

2. While dough is resting, finely dice 1 onion. (I like to use Vidalia onion when I can.) Mix with poppy seeds to taste.

3. After the dough has rested, cut out 3-oz/85.05-g pieces of dough.

4. Take each piece of dough and smash it down with your hand onto your work surface.

5. Then take your onion and poppy seed mixture and sprinkle it on the middle of the dough.

6. Fold in each edge of the dough on top of the onion and poppy seeds, similar to an envelope.

7. Dip the top (the seamless side of the roll) into the onion and poppy mixture as well.

8. Place on a parchment-lined baking sheet, seam side down.

9. Proof for 45 minutes. (Keep in mind that they will proof quickly because of the sugars in the onions.)

10. Bake for 25 minutes at 400°F/205°C, checking frequently throughout baking to make sure the onions on the top of the rolls don't burn.

Prepare the onions and poppy seed mixture ahead of time. This is the perfect recipe to experiment with flavors. You don't need to use onions, you can use shallots instead. Or instead of poppy seeds, you can make an onion and spicy pepper roll. You could do even do an "everything" onion pocket. Be creative and play around with shapes and sizes.

# SALT STICKS

---

Like our rye bread, these salt sticks have been around for generations. They are the Jewish version of the German pretzel. Many restaurants and beer halls love these because their salty nature encourages more consumption. Along with a beer or a Dr. Brown's cream soda, these rolls are perfect for your brisket, pastrami, or even steak dinner.

Makes approximately 40 salt sticks.

1.  Make one recipe of white bread dough (see page 122).

2.  After the dough has rested, remove from bowl onto floured workspace.

3.  Use your dough scraper to cut out 2-oz/56.7-g pieces of dough.

4.  Roll each piece, using the palm of your hand, into a ball shape, similar to the dinner roll technique on page 68.

5.  Press down in the center of the dough and roll it back and forth between your fingers and the work surface until it looks like a mini baguette, approximately 3 in/7.62 cm long.

6.  On another part of the counter, generously spread a mixture of 80 percent caraway seeds and 20 percent pretzel salt (or substitute kosher salt).

7.  Gently spray dough with water and roll it in caraway and salt mixture.

8.  Place shaped dough very close to one another on a parchment-lined baking sheet. (Keeping them close together, and letting them bake into one another, is what helps make these rolls soft.)

9.  Proof for 45 minutes. (Keep in mind that they will proof quickly.)

10. Bake for 25 minutes at 400°F/205°C.

# Sandwich Rectangles

Like our cibatta, these sandwich size rolls are delicious. I personally love them when I make paninis.
They toast up beautifully and are the perfect complement to hearty meats and savory cheeses.
Just like our burger buns, they freeze and keep well when placed in an airtight freezer bag.

Makes approximately 16 sandwich rectangles.

1. Make one batch of ciabatta dough (see page 133).
2. Place on a lightly floured work surface.
3. Using all of your fingers, push the dough down repeatedly so that it spreads. Continue this process until the dough is approximately .5 in/1.25 cm thick.
4. Using a pizza cutter, cut dough into rectangles that are approximately 1.5 in/4 cm by 5 in/13 cm in size.
5. Place on a parchment-lined baking sheet.
6. Lightly dust with flour.
7. Bake at 400°F/205°C for 30 minutes.

# Pumpernickel Rolls

---

These little dark rolls are richly flavored with coffee, molasses, raisins, and walnuts.

Makes approximately 36 rolls.

1. Make one batch of pumpernickel dough (see page 127) up through step 10.

2. Use your dough scraper to cut out 2-oz/56.7-g pieces of dough.

3. Shape into dinner rolls (see page 68).

4. Place rolls on a parchment-lined baking sheet.

5. Let dough rest 3 hours after shaping.

6. Preheat oven to 440°F/225°C.

7. Bake for 20 minutes.

# WHOLE-WHEAT ROLLS

Since a recipe of whole-wheat bread makes 5 pounds of dough, you can make a couple of loaves of bread and some rolls all from one batch.

Makes approximately 40 rolls

1. Make one batch of whole-wheat dough (see page 118) up through step 10.
2. Use your dough scraper to cut out 1.75-oz/50.18-g pieces of dough.
3. Shape into dinner rolls (see page 68).
4. Place rolls on a parchment-lined baking sheet.
5. Let dough rest 2 hours after shaping.
6. Preheat oven to 410°F/210°C.
7. Bake for 20 minutes, until the crust is golden.

# Chapter 6

# ARTISAN WINE AND BEER BREADS

Perhaps one of the most interesting and exciting new ventures I have embarked on since purchasing Orwashers has been the creation of our artisan wine and beer breads. When I began to revitalize the bakery, I searched for a product that was unique, that no other New York City bakers were doing at the time. For inspiration, I looked—where else? The past. But this time I went way back, to the original bread bakers: the Egyptians.

Historically speaking, wine and beer have been associated with bread leavening from as far back as biblical times. In ancient Egypt, the wine-making facilities and the bread-making facilities would often be in the same room. In this setting it is said that a happy accident occurred: the yeast from the alcohol seeped into the air and, subsequently, into the dough that had been left to rest or proof and it caused the dough to rise. I like to think of wine, bread, and cheese as a "trinity." They each go through an aging process with mold and fermentation of sorts. There is a direct relationship between this process of yeast and mold and the art of each of their preparations, which is what makes the pairing of wine and bread and cheese so organic.

Channing Daugthers Vineyard grows a wide variety of grapes including Chardonnay, Pinot Grigio, Merlot, and Pinot Noir.

Keith at the vineyard helping to choose the grapes for his wine starter.

Some of the wine breads we have created at Orwashers.

# WINE BREADS

Given my involvement in the promotion of the local food movement, once I decided to pursue a line of wine breads, I wanted to choose a vineyard close to home. Long Island grapes, and wines for that matter, have really matured in the past two decades to produce local wines that in some cases rival California's. So I approached the Long Island Wine Council. Since my product relies heavily on fermentation, I wanted to team up with another artisan "fermenter." This was what brought me to explore the Channing Daughters Winery, and my partnership with winemaker Christopher Tracy. Channing Daughters Winery grows a wide variety of grapes, including Chardonnay, Pinot Grigio, Tocai Friulano, Sauvignon Blanc, Muscat Ottonel, Malvasia, Gewurztraminer, Pinot Bianco, Merlot, Blaufränkisch, Pinot Noir, Dornfelder, Cabernet Franc, and Cabernet Sauvignon, and they are growing new grapes and developing new wines all the time. The vineyard is located in Bridgehampton, NY, on a twenty-five-acre lot of land that boasts rows of vineyards, a small winery, and a tasting room. Channing Daughters was a prime choice for a partnership with Orwashers, not only because of their vast array of grapes, but because of their commitment to quality and artisanal experimentation. Just like Orwashers, Channing Daughters makes it a point to push the limits of their grapes and what they can do, creating a wide variety of special blended wines made from not only commercial yeast, but from wild yeast as well. They seek to create wines that will accompany every mood, type of food, occasion, and season.

When I first met with Chris Tracy, partner and winemaker at Channing Daughters, I could tell he was excited about my ideas to create preferments using vintages of their grapes. They do a lot of blending in their wine making, so taking this next step into bread was a logical progression. Christopher is also a chef, so he understands good food and the importance of bread on the table, and the role bread plays in a meal. Christopher was very open-minded about the project, which allowed us to really experiment and think outside the box. As a winemaker, the whole fermentation process is really exciting to him, whether it is happening at the vineyard or the bakery. Of course, as a winemaker, his grapes are very important to him. You could say he is somewhat of a horticulturist. His expertise in terms of how weather plays into a grape harvest was invaluable to me when trying to figure out which grapes would be ideal for any given bread.

Being able to go to the vineyard and pick the grapes I wanted—rich fruit that was loaded with this beautiful, natural Long Island yeast—was almost a spiritual experience for me. It was so rewarding to be in on the fermentation process from the ground floor. Not only was I able to pick and choose the grapes myself, but I could see where they were growing, get to know the land, see this part of the local movement in its glory, and be a part of keeping it alive and successful. The focus for the process of creating the wine starter was the concept of going back to basics and using what nature provided us, rather than a focus on the particular strain of grape. This is why, although I ultimately chose to use the Cabernet Sauvignon and Chardonnay grape strains, other strains of grapes would also work perfectly well to create a starter. The starter is not as much about the flavor extracted from the grape as it is about the natural flavor that develops from the yeast on the skins of the wine grapes. Although there is no documentation on the types of yeasts in the air on Long Island and how they may or may not affect the grapes, it has been proven over time that the local air and climate of any location has effects on many aspects of the products it produces. For example, there is documentation that the yeast in the air in San Francisco is very specific to that region, which is why San Francisco sourdough is so special and impossible to replicate. Therefore, I can only conclude that the environment on Long Island where Channing Daughters grows its delicious grapes has played a part in creating the types of yeasts that grow on the grapes' skins. That allows the yeasts to develop the unique flavors that go into my wine bread starters, and more importantly, into my wine breads. This is what local producers and food providers offer to artisans like me—and it is, in essence, what defines an artisanal product. As a result, I know my customers will enjoy a unique taste experience.

Initially, Chris and I were both unsure of how this project would turn out, but six years later, we are proud of where we started and where it has gone. I would like to think that my wine breads have become a staple at the vineyard. We send our breads to Channing Daughters every week to be served in the tasting room for their events. Tasting our wine breads has become part of the experience of visiting Channing Daughters, and I hope it will remain as such for years to come.

*"Being able to go to the vineyard and pick the grapes I wanted—rich fruit that was loaded with this beautiful, natural Long Island yeast—was almost a spiritual experience for me."*

## WINE STARTERS

Using a wine starter is a wonderful way to create a preferment for many reasons. Inherently, grapes have a lot of natural yeast on their skins; this is what allows the culture that is created for the starters to taste robust and fruitful. They are an integral part of our wine breads, beer breads, and our starters in general. Before I journeyed down the road of wine bread production we did not use wine in any of our prefermented breads. Afterward, we transitioned most of our starters to have a wine grape beginning. However, even though nearly all the breads we make at the bakery use wine grape starters, they are not what I would call "wine breads." Wine breads are created with a focus on the starter and the wine grape yeast that grows on the grape. They are special because they showcase the special flavors that come about from using a natural yeast.

As mentioned earlier, we refresh our starters every year to ensure their authenticity and purity, and this holds true for our wine starters as well. Every year we go to the vineyard and pick a fresh batch of grapes for new, vintage starters. When I first decided to pursue wine breads I wasn't sure how to pair the grapes with the breads. I felt that the Chardonnay grapes would have a nice nuance for the miche because of their light color and flavor. I wanted to think outside the bread, and balance the dark grapes with the lighter wheat bread and vice versa. The levain for the Cabernet starter retains a reddish hue for months. The bread doesn't have a red color, but when baking the bread you will see the slightest hint that this was once a wine grape. These are things you hope to be able to spot over time. As you become more experienced at making starters, you will start to experiment too. Whether it's with grapes from your own local vineyard or any other local produce, I fully encourage you too to think outside the box and develop your own starter recipes!

## WHAT ARE THE VARIETIES OF GRAPES I USE IN MY WINE BREADS?

Grapes are grown in many different varieties, each with its own taste. The grapes we chose, both Cabernet and Chardonnay, represent each end of the wine-making spectrum. The former is very dark, while the latter is very light. (Merlot or Sauvignon Blanc are also good candidates to use when creating a natural yeast).

## CHARDONNAY GRAPE

The Chardonnay grape is a green grape used to make white wines. It is also used to make sparkling wines, like champagne. It is an easily adaptable plant, so it grows in many different countries and states in the United States. Chardonnay is an extremely versatile grape because its taste really reflects that of the area in which it is being grown. It is because of this versatility that the Chardonnay grape is known as the winemaker's grape. The way the wine is made plays a larger role in what the wine will taste like than any intrinsic tastes or properties of the Chardonnay grape itself.

## CABERNET SAUVIGNON GRAPE

The Cabernet Sauvignon grape is a dark, purple grape that is used to make red wines. It is the most widely planted red-wine grape, and grows nearly all over the world. It is also quite adaptable to various soil types and climates. This grape comes from the Bordeaux country in France, and is a cross between two other known Bordeaux grapes, the Cabernet Franc and the Sauvignon Blanc. It is one of the most popular red grapes being grown and harvested today.

Christopher Tracy at Channing Daughters Vineyard overseeing the grape harvest.

# Q&A WITH CHRISTOPHER TRACY OF CHANNING DAUGHTERS:

## WHAT HAVE YOU LEARNED FROM WORKING WITH KEITH ON THIS JOINT EFFORT?

I have learned about the versatility of yeast and the value of great bread. My work with him has solidified my belief in multidisciplinary creative collaborations, not to mention how much I like to barter.

## HOW DID YOU COME TO WORK WITH KEITH?

Keith reached out to us initially and we thought wine bread was a super cool idea. Ancient and modern all at once, like so much of what we do here. Plus we love bread and can't get enough of it! We love telling the story of our place and creating delicious things that reflect where we are and where we came from. The bread project is another great example of this.

## WHAT WINES OF YOURS DOES KEITH USE IN HIS BREADS? WHY DID YOU AND KEITH CHOOSE THESE PARTICULAR WINES?

We generally use Chardonnay grapes and Cabernet Sauvignon grapes, not the wines. The reason for this is that we want the yeast present on the bloom of the grapes. Sometimes we use a bit of fermenting must that was fermenting wild (ambiently). Keith originally asked for these varieties, I think.

## WHAT IS YOUR OWN PHILOSOPHY ON ARTISAN PRODUCTS?

That is what we do. We strive to make something that is delicious and reflects our place. We try to do that as simply as possible with the least impact on our environment. I believe focusing on locally produced sustainable foods helps solve many of the problems in our modern world.

# BEER BREADS

The first beer makers were Egyptian, as well. Throughout history, beer has been seen as a healthful beverage, full of nutrients. Beer uses cereal grains, so to me it seemed a natural extension when I started to think of new ingredients to use in my breads.

When I began my search for a brewer, Sixpoint Brewery came to mind almost immediately. I wanted to use a real artisan beer maker that was local and focused on the community in a way that aligned with Orwashers philosophy. Sixpoint is a small, local beer maker based in Brooklyn, New York. They experiment with new things all the time, which is something we as artisans have in common. While Sixpoint isn't a particularly old company, having been founded in 2004, its roots are in the history of fermenting cereal grains. Just like the breads at Orwashers, Sixpoint beers also embody history and tradition.

Sixpoint set up shop in a 600-square-foot garage, which used to be an old brewery. They have since updated the space to current standards. Similar to my own philosophy, the creators of Sixpoint find inspiration in the past. They also are committed to building on beer's original health benefits. These like-minded intentions and shared common ground led to the birth of the Craft Ale Bread.

The product of the collaboration with Sixpoint is our Craft Ale Bread.

# Q&A WITH JEFF GORLECHEN
# AT SIXPOINT BREWERY:

### WHAT HAVE YOU LEARNED FROM WORKING WITH KEITH ON THIS JOINT EFFORT?
Keith is a creative baker and has done an impressive job of maintaining his company's tradition while also looking for innovative ways to keep his product current.

### HOW DID YOU COME TO WORK WITH KEITH?
The two of us met at a beer and food event in late 2009. We talked about doing a bread with Sixpoint beer, and the ideas started flowing.

### WHAT BEER OF YOURS DOES KEITH USE IN HIS BREADS? WHY DID YOU AND KEITH CHOOSE THESE PARTICULAR TYPES OF BEER?
The Otis oatmeal stout was chosen because of its use of flaked oats in the beer recipe. It also isn't particularly hoppy. We have also used Brownstone Ale and have discussed using the Righteous Ale and Autumnation Ale.

### WHAT WAS THE PROCESS LIKE OF DISCOVERING WHAT DID AND DIDN'T WORK FOR KEITH?
We kind of hit on the Otis right away; it seemed a good fit for what Keith wanted to do. We left it to Keith to figure out the proper amount of beer to use in the recipe. I think it took him three to four batches to hone in on the right proportion, and it's been a huge success.

RIGHT A brewer at Sixpoint works on crafting one of the beers.

# Cabernet Rustica Bread

The moist, aerated interior of this bread has a complex and slightly sour flavor profile and a hearty, crisp crust. The final product is destined for dipping in olive oils and accompanying your dinner every night of the week.

Makes 4 loaves.

2.23 lbs/1 kg bread flour  *100%*

1.48 lbs/671.3 g water  *67%*

1.03 lbs/467.2 g levain  *46.7%*
   (see below)

.02 lb/9.1 g instant yeast  *.91%*

.08 lb/36.3 g salt  *3.6%*

Levain:

3 lbs/1.36 kg mother  *348%*
   (see page 108)

1.14 lbs/ 517.1 g water  *132%*

.86 lb/390.1 g white flour  *100%*

1.  Set up stand mixer with a dough hook.
2.  Place flour, water, levain, and yeast in the mixing bowl.
3.  Mix on medium-low for 2 minutes.
4.  Add salt and mix on medium for 3 minutes.
5.  Dough should appear shiny and will pull away from the mixing bowl.
6.  Do the dough test (see page 47).
7.  Let the dough rest for 15 minutes.
8.  Mix dough on low speed for 1 minute.
9.  Transfer to lightly oiled airtight container and let rest for 1 hour.
10. Fold dough (see page 59).
11. Let dough rest on countertop for approximately 2 additional hours. Dough should double in size.
12. Roll dough out of container onto a floured work surface (marble or butcher block is ideal).
13. Cut dough with a scraper into 4 even squares/rectangles, approximately 1.5 lbs/680.4 g each.
14. Shape each into rustic free-form (see page 65).
15. Dust with flour and let rest for about 1 hour.
16. Preheat oven to 480°F/250°C with baking stone inside.
17. About 1 minute prior to putting loaves in oven, spray baking stone with water to create steam.
18. Turn loaves over and place them on peel; then use peel to load bread onto the stone.
19. Spray sides of oven again with water to create another burst of steam.
20. Bake for 45 minutes.

Handle (minimally) with care: For the lightest, airiest bread, this dough should be handled as little as possible. Lightly flour your hands and move the dough the least amount possible during the folding and shaping stage.

# CABERNET SESAMO BREAD

For a crunchy change of pace, try this variation of Cabernet rustica
that includes the addition of sesame seeds.

Makes 4 loaves.

1. Make Cabernet rustica dough (see page 182) up through step 13.
2. Shape each into rustic free-form (see page 65).
3. On another part of the counter, generously sprinkle sesame seeds.
4. After shaping the dough, gently spray it with water.
5. Once damp, gently roll dough into sesame seeds, making sure to cover the entire bread.
6. Move dough to your resting board. Cover and allow to proof.
7. Use the same oven temperature as for baking the Cabernet rustica (480°F/250°C) but bake the bread about 10 minutes longer to really toast the sesame seeds.

# Chardonnay Miche Bread

This bread boasts a dark-baked crust and a tangy, chewy interior. It is a hearty option to pair with soups and stews and a great accompaniment for cheese plates and artisan sandwiches.

Makes 4 loaves.

2.18 lbs/988.8 g bread flour    *100%*

.1 lb/45.36 g whole-wheat flour    *104%*

1.48 lbs/671.3 g water    *65%*

.5 lb/226.8 g dark rye starter    *22%*
    (see page 113)

.5 lb/226.8 g white starter    *22%*
    (see page 113)

.09 lb/40.82 g salt    *3.9%*

.01 lb/4.54 g instant yeast    *.43*

1. Set up stand mixer with a dough hook.
2. Place bread flour, whole-wheat flour, and water in mixing bowl.
3. Mix on low until combined.
4. Cover bowl with a damp cloth or towel, and let rest for 15 minutes.
5. Add dark rye starter, white starter, salt, and yeast to mixing bowl.
6. Mix on medium-low for 4 minutes.
7. Mix on medium-high for 11 minutes.
8. Dough should appear shiny and pull away from your mixing bowl.
9. Do the dough test (see page 47).
10. Take dough out of mixing bowl and transfer to lightly oiled airtight container.
11. Let dough rest in container for 1 hour.
12. Fold (see page 59) and put back in container.
13. Let dough rest on countertop for approximately 4 hours. Dough should double in size.
14. Roll dough out of container onto a lightly floured work surface (marble or butcher block is ideal).
15. Cut dough with a scraper into 4 even squares/rectangles, approximately 1.5 lbs/680.4 g each.
16. Shape each into boule (see page 60).
17. Let dough proof for 4 hours.
18. Preheat oven to 480°F/250C.
19. Bake for 50 minutes until crust is dark and well baked.

# MICHE ROLLS

---

Same dough, different shape, makes for a lovely dinner or sandwich roll.

Makes approximately 24 rolls.

1. Make one batch of Chardonnay miche dough through step 13 (see page 186).

2. Use your dough scraper to cut out 4-oz/113.4-g pieces of dough.

3. Shape into dinner rolls (see page 68).

4. Place rolls on a parchment-lined baking sheet.

5. Proof for 45 minutes to an hour.

6. Top with a dusting of flour.

7. Score the top of the rolls with a small "X" approximately 1 in/2.5 cm by 1 in/2.5 cm.

8. Let the rolls rest for a few minutes before you put them in the oven.

9. Bake at 450°F/230°C for 25 minutes.

# RUSTIC WINE ROLLS

These hearty rolls are great with stew or a thick soup.

Makes approximately 48 rolls.

1.  Make one batch of Cabernet rustica dough through step 12 (see page 182).

2.  Use dough scraper to cut out 2-oz/56.7-g pieces of dough. Shape into rustic rolls (see page 69).

3.  Place rolls on a parchment-lined baking sheet for softer rolls, or on a baking stone for crustier rolls.

4.  Top with a dusting of flour.

5.  Proof rolls for 30-45 minutes. (These rolls may need less time to proof, if the dough was cut with only a small amount of handling. Keep an eye on them; when they have increased about 50% in size, they are ready for the oven.)

6.  Bake at 450°F/230°C for 25 minutes.

# CRAFT ALE BREAD

By pouring beer directly into the dough before baking this loaf, you are adding in a malty, sour flavor that develops in the fermentation period. The result is a crusty bread with an airy interior and a bold, slightly sour taste; the beer bread is perfect for a grilled cheese sandwich or for dipping in olive oil.

Makes 4 loaves.

2.1 lbs/952.5 g spring flour *100%* *1065*

.25 lb/113.4 g whole-wheat flour

1.28 lbs/580.6 g water *54.5%*

.5 lb/226.8 g dark rye starter *21.29%*
    (see page 113)

.3 lb/136.1 g whole-wheat biga *12.77%*
    (see page 113)

.3 lb/136.1 g beer *12.77%*

.1 lb/45.36 g white starter *4.25%*
    (see page 113)

.06 lb/27.22 g salt *2.55%*

.004 lb/1.81 g instant yeast *.169%*

1. Set up stand mixer with a dough hook.
2. Place spring flour, whole-wheat flour, and water in mixing bowl.
3. Mix on low until combined.
4. Cover bowl with a damp cloth, or towel, and let rest for 10 minutes
5. Add dark rye starter, whole-wheat biga, beer, white starter, salt, and yeast to mixing bowl.
6. Mix on medium-low for 4 minutes.
7. Mix on high for 8 minutes.
8. Dough should appear shiny and pull away from the mixing bowl.
9. Do the dough test (see page 47).
10. Take dough out of mixing bowl and transfer to lightly oiled airtight container.
11. Let dough rest on countertop for approximately 3 hours. Dough should double in size.
12. Roll dough out of container onto a lightly floured work surface (marble or butcher block is ideal).
13. Cut dough with a scraper into 4 even squares/rectangles, approximately 1.5 lbs/680.4 g each.
14. Shape each into a boule (see page 60).
15. Let dough proof for 4 hours.
16. Preheat oven to 480°F/250°C.
17. Score a spiral into the dough.
18. Bake for 55 minutes until crust is dark and well baked.

# Corn Rye Bread

Corn rye is a spin-off of our traditional New York rye bread. This version is slightly peppery and much denser than the original, making it the perfect twist for your pastrami or corned beef sandwich.

Makes 4 loaves.

1.93 lbs/875.4 g white flour — 100% 875

1.75 lbs/793.8 g white rye biga — 90% (see page 113)

.94 lb/426.4 g water — 45.7%

.25 lb/113.4 g beer — 12.96%

.03 lb/13.61 g caraway seeds — 1.55%

.08 lb/36.29 g salt — 4.14%

.03 lb/13.61 g instant yeast — 1.55%

1. Set up stand mixer with a dough hook.
2. Place flour, rye biga, water, beer, caraway seeds, salt, and yeast in mixing bowl.
3. Mix on medium-low for 4 minutes.
4. Mix on high for 7 minutes.
5. Dough should appear shiny and pull away from the mixing bowl.
6. Do the dough test (see page 47).
7. Take dough out of mixing bowl and transfer to lightly oiled airtight container.
8. Let dough rest on countertop for approximately 2 hours. Dough should double in size.
9. Roll dough out of container onto a lightly floured work surface (marble or butcher block is ideal).
10. Cut dough with a scraper into 4 even squares/rectangles, approximately 1.5 lbs/680.4 g each.
11. Shape each into a boule (see page 60).
12. Let dough rest 6 hours after shaping.
13. Preheat oven to 490°F/255°C.
14. Bake for 55 minutes until crust is dark and well baked.

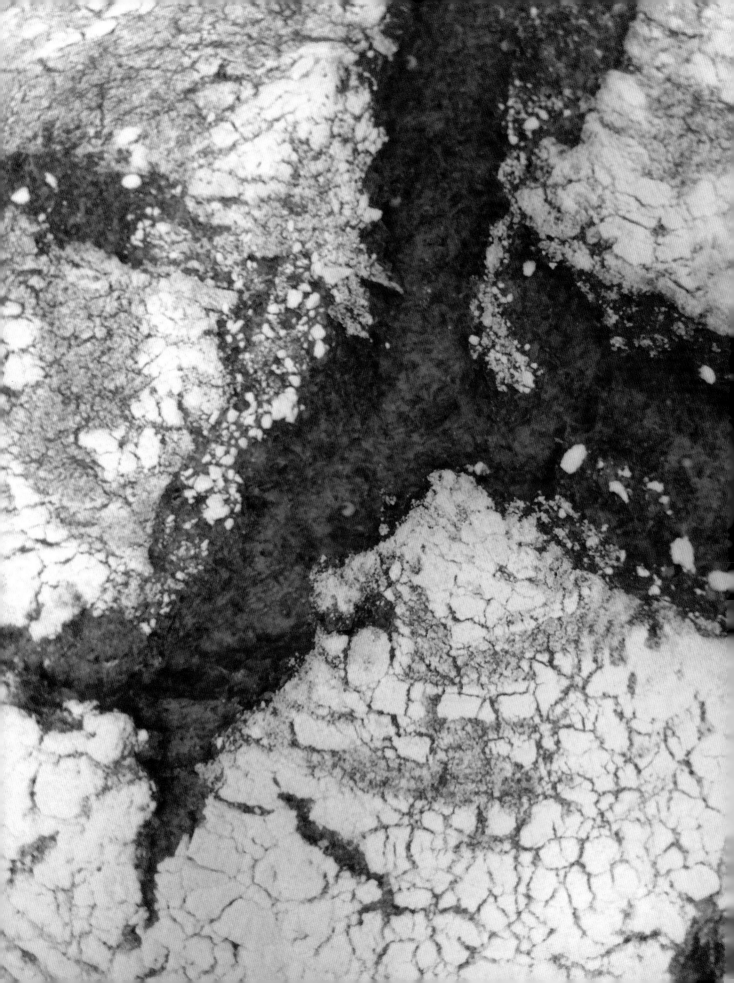

# Chapter 7

# EXPERIMENTATION AND TROUBLESHOOTING

Part of what makes baking so interesting is the amount of experimentation you can do. This is where Baker's Math will really come in handy. After baking many times while following a recipe, you will begin to get a sense of how the flour you are using reacts to water, how long it takes the yeast or preferment you are using to ferment and rise, and how your oven works. Once you have a handle on those factors, that's when the real fun begins! You can feel free to go off script, so to speak, and improvise with different ingredients and methods. Ideas can come from anywhere. The great thing about most of these recipes is that they can all be altered and changed as long as you can master the Baker's Math formula and keep the ratios in proportion.

For example, you may want to try substituting milk for water to give your bread additional richness. However, milk that has not been scalded contains a glutathione, an antioxidant that can weaken the gluten bonds in bread. Scalding your milk will help counteract this weakening effect. Most milk, liquid and powered, has not been scalded properly to 170°F to 180°F (77°C to 82°C). If it's not expressly written on the packaging, you should assume that it hasn't been and you should scald it yourself. Whole milk is made up of approximately 87 percent water (the rest is fat and protein). If you choose to substitute milk for water, you may need to add some extra water to get the amount of hydration needed in the dough. You can also try doing half milk and half water and adjusting until you get the consistency and flavor you prefer.

You can substitute whole-wheat flour in the Cabernet rustica if you would like a more health-conscious bread. You can play around by adding ingredients like nuts, olives, or raisins if you'd like to give a simpler bread a boost in taste. Recipes can be altered to be savory or sweet, depending on your needs. Focaccia especially is wonderful for this type of experimentation and variation. You can also combine flours. For example, if you want the added protein of bread flour and the added nutrients of whole grain, you can use some of both types. Just make sure that the two flours add up to the total amount of flour called for in the recipe.

There is only one rule in experimentation: remember or write down what you did so you can replicate it, or so you don't make the same mistake twice!

*"Once you have a handle on the basics you can feel free to improvise with different ingredients and methods."*

## SOLVING THE CABERNET RUSTICA MYSTERY

When I created the recipe for our Cabernet rustica, it took me weeks before I found the perfect balance of hydration, mixing, and shaping techniques. I would take a loaf fresh from the oven and cut into it, only to be disappointed by what I found. The problem was that the bread's cell structure was too tight; I wanted a beautifully open and airy bread with a sturdy, yet delicate crust. Yet day after day I tried and couldn't get it right. Eventually, I took a step back in time and thought about the origins of wine breads. I realized wine breads were created at a time in history when the monetary value of ingredients would have dictated their relative percentages in a recipe. Obviously water would have been less expensive than flour. I realized that I was underhydrating the dough. This improved the recipe, but it still wasn't perfect. I then took a look at our mixing and shaping techniques. They didn't have stand mixers back then, which made me realize we were probably handling the dough for too long and overmixing. When I cut down the mixing time significantly, everything fell into place, producing the beautiful loaf we make now.

Whether you are experimenting with different ingredients or following the recipes exactly, you are bound to encounter some problems along the way. Even seasoned bakers find that things go awry sometimes. You might find that your dough isn't rising enough during resting or proofing, or that it isn't rising enough in the oven. You may take your bread out of the oven, and after cooling, cut into it to discover the hole structure of the crumb isn't what you had hoped for, or the crust isn't crunchy enough. If this happens to you—and it is bound to happen at one point or another—you need to start retracing the baking process in your head to see where you might have gone wrong. *Is my starter alive? Did I remember to put the yeast in the dough? What was my final mixing temperature—was it too high or low?* Despite conscientious effort, sometimes the finished product doesn't come out quite as we planned. Baking is a type of discipline that you should have fun doing, but it can be frustrating at times. There will be days when you have your rhythm and your bread comes out perfectly, and other days when you just can't figure out why your bread is off. I can tell you that this is completely normal; as I have said, no matter how seasoned a baker a person is, we all have our off days. I encourage you all to keep with it, despite these down days. As you practice, you will get better at troubleshooting and you will produce more consistently perfect bread.

However, first you need to work on discovering what went wrong and what you should do about it. The tips in this section will serve as basic tools to help you fine-tune your recipes. They address some common troubleshooting problems and techniques to help you achieve your ideal bread. The best way to tackle troubleshooting is to keep notes and take educated guesses as to how you can fix the problem. If the first adjustment doesn't work, try another. You will get there eventually. There is no one right answer that I can give you, but experimenting and learning from your mistakes can be part of the fun!

The top loaf was proofed too long causing the dough to rise too much and then collapse. The lower loaf didn't proof enough and the result is a very dense, flat bread.

# PRE-BAKING CHECK LIST

Here are a few things you can check for BEFORE your bread goes into the oven. If you catch these potential problems ahead of time, you can still salvage your dough.

### CHECK TO MAKE SURE YOUR PREFERMENT (IF YOU'RE USING ONE) IS STILL ALIVE.

You want to see bubbles. It should be linen white or slightly creamy. You don't want it to look gray. The smell should cause you to cough a little bit; it will be a pungent, slightly acidic, "vinese" odor (kind of like vinegar or wine that's beginning to turn to vinegar). It should be powerful, but not stink. Unless you have an extremely sensitive gag reflex, if your starter makes you feel sick, then it has probably gone bad and you shouldn't use it. You can also tell if it has turned because it will be oily on top. Check the expiration date on your yeast, as well.

### CHECK YOUR FINAL MIXING TEMPERATURE.

As mentioned earlier, the final temperature for your mixed batch of dough should be between 72°F/22°C and 76°F/24°C. Anything much colder, it will take longer for the dough to proof. You run the risk of the dough starting to break down. If warmer, the dough will rise much more quickly and you won't be able to allow it to mature. Your final mixing temperatures shouldn't be a result of under- or overmixing the dough. (You are better off undermixing than overmixing.) If your final mixing temperature isn't right, you can try to compensate for this by altering your fermentation and proofing time. Remember, a colder dough will rise more slowly than a warmer dough, so adjust your time accordingly and make sure the dough doubles in size.

A very watery starter is a sign that it's no longer active.

### CHECK THE CONSISTENCY OF YOUR DOUGH AND MAKE SURE IT'S RIGHT.

If your dough is too sticky or soupy, you need to check your hydration rates. If you added too much water, you may need to add a little more flour to work the dough. If it's too dry, you can add water in very small amounts and work it into the dough. Be sure to check the temperature of the water you are adding. You also may have undermixed the dough. You can compensate for this through a series of folds. Repeat some of the folds you used when shaping this particular loaf until you achieve the right consistency.

### CHECK TO MAKE SURE YOU'VE SET A TIMER OR ARE KEEPING A CLOSE WATCH ON TIME FOR EACH STEP IN THE PROCESS.

If you don't keep track of when you start each stage of the process, you will most likely do something for too long. Everything should be precisely timed. You may need more or less time than is suggested in the recipe, but you won't ever know unless you are keeping track. One minute too long mixing or baking could make a huge difference in your final product.

### CHECK TO MAKE SURE YOUR PANS AREN'T FILLED UP TOO HIGH.

Your pans should be filled about two-thirds of the way up before baking. If they are filled too high, the bread will spill over the edges in the oven when it does its final rise. If you overshot this and your bread rose more than you anticipated during proofing, you can try to transfer the dough to a larger pan—although you must do it very carefully so as not to compromise the gluten strands you've created.

Bread that's blondish and very light should have been baked longer.

# POST-BAKING TROUBLESHOOTING

If your bread comes out of the oven and the outcome isn't what you expected, there isn't anything you can do to change the final product at this point. You can only study your loaf and learn from your mistakes. Here are some common things that may have gone wrong, why, and how you can make sure not to repeat the same mistake next time.

### THE LOAF DIDN'T RISE VERY MUCH IN THE OVEN.

There are several reasons why this might have occurred. You may not have used enough yeast in your dough. To avoid this, double check your percentages and make sure they are correct the next time. Your problem may also have to do with salt. Perhaps the yeast came in direct contact with the salt, therefore died off, or perhaps you used too much salt. Salt, as you know, can significantly slow down the yeast activity. Again, make sure that your salt percentages are accurate next time. This may also be the result of under- or overproofing. If you underproofed your dough, you didn't give the gluten enough time to form or the yeast enough time to produce the gas for the holes. If you overproofed your dough, the yeast may have lost its momentum and the gluten will not be able to support the further rise of the loaf.

### THE LOAF IS POORLY SHAPED, OR HAD TOO BIG AN "OVEN SPRING."

If your loaf didn't hold its shape after baking, that could mean that you overproofed the dough, causing the yeast to be overworked so the gluten can no longer support the structure. This could also be the fault of overfilling your pan, if you are using one. If your dough had a very large—almost too-large—oven spring this could be the result of underproofing. If your dough wasn't left out long enough for the yeast to do its work before baking, when it goes into the oven the yeast will be so overactive that it may cause your bread to overexpand.

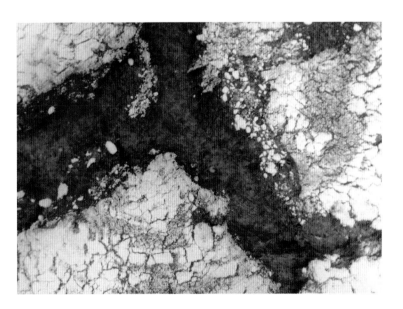

These irregular, torn-looking scores are a sign that the bread proofed too long.

## BREAD TASTES SOUR OR HAS A STRONG ODOR.

This could be the result of overproofing. Be sure to perform the finger test (see page 70) to make sure the dough is ripe. The dough should almost double in size when proofing, but it should not rise beyond that. You could have also underbaked your dough, or used too much yeast.

## THE SCORES ON THE CRUST DIDN'T OPEN.

There are a few possible reasons for why cuts don't open. First, the dough may have been too slack—meaning it could have been too wet. Second, it might not have been shaped tightly enough. A third possibility is that perhaps you didn't score your dough deeply enough. Scoring the bread is an art; it can take several tries to get it right. Don't lose faith!

## THE CRUST IS TOO HARD OR TOO THICK.

If your crust is too hard, it's possible that you have overbaked the bread. If it is a challenge to get your oven to the high temperatures suggested in the recipes, you may have over compensated for the temperature by leaving the bread in for too long, resulting in a crust that is too tough. You also may have underhydrated your dough, or it may not have been protected correctly during proofing and therefore the skin dried out.

## THE CRUST ISN'T THE RIGHT COLOR.

If the crust is too dark, a few things may have happened. You may have overbaked the bread, or the temperature in your oven may be too high. If neither one of those things seems likely, then you may have put too much sugar in the dough. If the crust is only too dark on the top or bottom, you probably have the loaf positioned too high or too low in the oven. If the crust is too pale, you may not have let the dough bake long enough, or your oven temperature was too low. Your dough may also have dried out during proofing, resulting in not enough moisture to activate the caramelization of the crust.

A lopsided or misshapen loaf means that either too much yeast was used or that the bread didn't proof long enough so that the heat from the oven caused it to rise too quickly and unevenly.

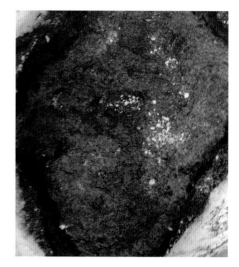

An overly dark crust means the bread was overbaked or there was too much sugar in the dough.

## THE CRUMB HAS NO HOLES.

A lack of holes can be caused by overmixing or underhydrating. When you underhydrate the dough, the cell structure looks completely different. If your bread comes out of the oven without enough holes, be sure to monitor your mixing and hydrating more carefully in the next batch to compensate for this problem.

## THE CRUMB IS GUMMY.

You may not have baked the bread long enough. Or your oven temperature was too hot—if you bake the crust too quickly, it gets hard and brown, and you might end up taking the bread out of the oven before the center is baked through. You could also have sliced into it before it was fully done cooling.

## THE CRUMB HAS HOLES THAT ARE TOO LARGE.

You may have overproofed the dough. Always perform the finger test (see page 70). You also may have shaped the bread incorrectly, without punching down enough so too much gas remained in the dough.

Of course, sometimes, despite best effort and careful analysis, the bread just won't come out right. Chalk it up to the weather, or a bad batch of one of your ingredients, or something equally inexplicable. Take notes, try again. Practice will actually make perfect.

If the holes in the crumb are too large or the bread is falling apart it may be a sign that the bread was overproofed or that you didn't get enough of the gas out of the dough during the punching down stage.

Very few or no holes in bread means it was overmixed or didn't have enough liquid.

# Chapter 8

# Orwashers and Artisan Breads— Our Latest Challenge

As an artisan, I am constantly searching for ways to improve my craft. No matter how good you are at what you do, there are always ways to make something better, purer, closer to perfect. There is always something you can learn from someone else's techniques and philosophies that will inform your own process. Therefore, in July of 2013, I ventured off to the "promised land" of bread—Paris, France—to continue my baking education.

My goal was to master the national bread of France, the baguette. This may seem like a rudimentary task—making a bread that I should have mastered long ago. However, you will be surprised to learn that the baguette is the most complex bread out there. Part of its complexity lies in the fact that it seems so simple; it is something of a paradox. Unfortunately, this is not the first time I've encountered this type of conundrum. Back in high school, I played tennis. In order to be cool, I adopted a Western, heavy, topspin-style grip—a rather advanced swing. To my chagrin, despite being able to perform this difficult swing, I was still unable to hit a simple flat stroke! And so, as you may imagine, my tennis career came to a halt; but I refused to let the same thing happen to my baking. I knew we at Orwashers could bake an authentic French baguette, and I knew we could get it right by being true to tradition—the same approach I took to rebuilding Orwashers into one of the city's best bakeshops. And so, off to Paris I went!

I stayed a total of ten days in France, four of which were spent at Viron Mill, a small mill with an attached bakery in Chartres, about fifty miles outside of Paris. The rest of the time I spent in Paris, working along some of the best French bakers in the world.

At Viron, I worked closely with, and studied from, the famous artisan and baker Raoul Maeder, who is known for his award-winning baguettes. It was an eye-opening experience just to see how these bakers work, and where their techniques are similar to, and where they differ from, ours in the United States.

The milling method is similar to the mills I work with at home: a lot attention goes into blending the flours to achieve consistency

## GOT BREAD?

Interestingly, even though bread has traditionally been an integral part of the French diet, lately there has been a pull away from bread there. The bad reputation that bread has here in the United States has finally reached France. People are eating less bread than they used to, and the Bread Bakers Association is currently promoting bread in a campaign that is similar to the "Got Milk?" campaign that ran here in the United States, but is essentially "Got Bread?" The association is putting advertisements in the windows of French bakeries and attempting to educate the public on the benefits of bread.

throughout the growing season and year to year. The type of flour used for the baguette is what the French call a "type 55 flour." It has a protein content of about 10.8 percent. At Viron Mill, I and other bakers were working with their head baker in a "classroom" setting in their test bakery. It was great to be able to immerse myself totally in the learning process in a pure environment, without retail pressures. After learning the technique at the test bakery, we moved to a small retail bakery in Chartres for a few days and then to the big-city Parisian bakeries. Seeing the "real-world" bakeries in Paris gave me the confidence that we could make master top-quality baguette production while dealing with the rigors of a busy retail shop. I would equate the whole experience to learning to throw a baseball into the strike zone while you are pitching to your dad (working in the test bakery), versus pitching inside a stadium with 50,000 fans screaming at you (baking baguettes in a bustling Parisian retail bakery).

When it comes to dough development, French bakers use time as their friend—just as bakers used to do in ancient times. They allow the dough to rest for more time than we do here in the United States. They are also gentler with their dough. They opt to mix their dough on high for a minute or two, instead of mixing for a longer time on low; and immediately after they finish mixing, they let the dough rest for an hour in the bowl. Only after it has rested do they finish the mixing and, as mentioned, they do so for a shorter amount of time than a similar American recipe would suggest. While this method works very well in a smaller French bakery that is producing a maximum of four or five different types of bread, it isn't feasible when working in a wholesale bakery, which caters to the needs of many restaurants and clients.

As a home baker, however, you can easily experiment with this method, particularly when baking some of the recipes in this book. I encourage you to mix for a minute on high and let the dough rest in the bowl for fifteen minutes, then mix on high again but for less time than the original recipe calls for. Experiment with this a bit and see how it influences your finished product. Just make sure to document what you do so you can keep track of the effects

*"My goal was to learn to create baguettes that are of the same taste and quality that you'd find at a great French bakery."*

Keith in the test kitchen at Chartes where he made hundreds of baguettes.

Keith with award-winning French baker, Raoul Maeder.

your methods have on your breads. That way, you can determine whether or not you have effectively adjusted the recipe to make a more "French"-style loaf, if that is what you aspire to do.

For us at the bakery, however, what I brought back was the traditional knowledge and methods of the French bakers, which enabled me to develop our own baguette that will work in the French tradition in a retail setting here. We were even accompanied back to New York by a member of the Retroder baking family, who then worked with us at Orwashers for two weeks to ensure that we were carrying out the French technique properly. This enlightening trip inspired our brand-new creation, the Baguette Traditionelle, which uses traditional French flour and is baked using the same process as the "baguette de tradition française." We knew it would be a challenge, but one that matched our sensibilities and the processes we already had in place. As a hundred- year-old bakery already practicing traditional baking methods, it was only a matter of finding the right flour and the right partners to create baguettes that are of the same taste and quality that you'd find at a great French bakery.

On the plane ride home from France, as I reflected on the time I had spent abroad, I was energized and truly inspired to create new recipes and rework some of the old ones. The French have so much respect for their food, and most importantly their bread. There has been a huge resurgence here in the states on eating fresh, local, and healthier foods. I want to be at the forefront of this movement by staying true to my vision for artisan breads. I encourage the reader, when possible, to use local flours and to really get to know a recipe's ingredients. The purpose of this book is not necessarily to give you cookie-cutter step-by-step instructions. Bread isn't like that. The purpose is to help inspire you, give you guidance and a solid foundation in the basics, and to evoke your creativity. Remember, a good baker never stops learning.

# Baguette

The intensive training in France resulted in this authentic tasting light and airy loaf
with a golden crunchy crust. It's a little bit of Paris here in the U.S.

Makes 7 loaves.

2.9 lbs/1.32 kg flour

1.98 lbs/898 g water

.08 lb/36.29 g salt

.02 lb/.57 g instant yeast

1. Set up stand mixer with a dough hook.
2. Place flour, water, salt, and yeast in mixing bowl.
3. Mix on medium for 8 minutes.
4. Allow dough to rest in the bowl for 1 hour.
5. Take dough out of mixing bowl and transfer to lightly oiled airtight container.
6. Let dough rest on countertop for approximately 1 hour.
7. Fold dough (see page 59).
8. Refrigerate dough for at least 18 but no more than 30 hours.
9. Remove from refrigerator and rest on the counter for approximately 1 hour or until you notice the dough rising.
10. Divide dough into 6 12-oz/340.2-g pieces and 1 6-oz/170.1 g pieces.
11. Let rest on counter for approximately 20 minutes or until you see the dough starting to relax and show some bubbles.
12. Shape the dough (see page 214).
13. Let dough rest for 20 minutes after shaping.
14. Preheat oven to 500°F/260°C.
15. Score bageuttes with 4-5 slashes.
16. Spray a good amount of water inside the oven before and after you put the bread in to bake. Steam is key to the success of this bread.
16. Bake for 22-26 minutes until crust is gold brown.

**BAGUETTE SHAPING**

The baguette is traditionally one of the hardest breads to shape.

1. Place an individual piece of dough on a lightly floured work surface.

2. Gently pat the dough out to a rectangle, approximately 10 in/25 cm by 8 in/20 cm.

3. Fold the top third of the dough down towards the middle.

4. Fold the bottom third of the dough up towards the middle and use the heels of your palms to seal the seam.

5. Flip the dough, so the seam is on the bottom, and gently roll between the palm of your hand and the work surface. Be sure to start in the middle and slowly work your way to the ends. The dough should be even throughout. Roll until the dough is slightly shorter than the length of your sheet pan.

6. Let the dough rest for approximately 30-45 minutes on a lightly floured cloth or a linen kitchen towel. Make sure your baguettes are not touching by tucking folds of the cloth around the baguettes.

7. Once dough has roughly doubled in size, transfer to a baking stone.

## SHAPING TIP:

The key to proper baguette shaping is in the handling of the dough. You need a gentle hand to make sure you don't degass the dough too much or you won't get the airy crumb but you need to be firm enough to make sure it's rolled tightly to hold its shape. The only way to master this shaping technique is to practice, practice, practice.

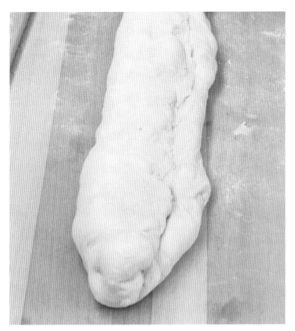

Step 1

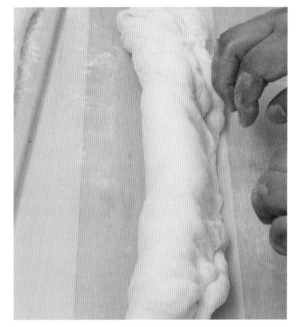

Step 3

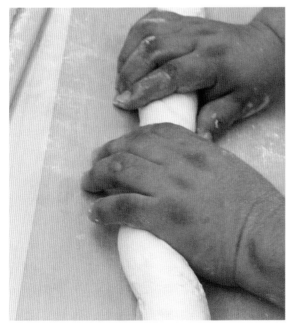

Step 5

Step 6

# GLOSSARY

**Autolyse:** The French technique by which you combine the flour and water first and let the mixture sit for twenty or thirty minutes before adding in the salt and other ingredients.

**Baker's Math:** This is the formula by which all of the ingredients in a given recipe are turned into ratios based on their relation to flour. Flour always equals 100% in the Baker's Math formula.

**Bigas:** A type of stiff preferment that is made from one quarter water and three quarters flour, and some yeast.

**Boule:** French word for "ball," used to describe a round loaf shape.

**Caramelize:** The reaction that occurs during baking where the sugars oxidize and turn brown.

**Cooling:** The term used to describe the bread left out to cool after it has been baked.

**Crumb:** The interior of the bread.

**Crust:** The outer layer of the bread.

**Crystallize:** The reaction that occurs when the bread is left to cool in an environment that is too cold; the starch cells in the bread are forced to absorb whatever water they can find, which traps and hardens them.

**Elasticity:** The term used to describe the stretchiness of the dough, or its ability to snap back after being shaped.

**Enriched bread:** Breads that have added fats and sugars from ingredients like eggs, butter, and milk.

**Enriched flour:** Flour that has had some of the vitamins and nutrients lost during the milling process added back into the final product.

**Extensibility:** The term used to describe the dough's ability to expand and be shaped.

**Gelatinize:** The reaction that occurs when the heat from the oven causes the starch molecules to absorb as much moisture as possible, forcing them to swell and then explode. The liquid that comes out thickens and forms a gelatin coating that hardens into the crust.

**Gluten:** The protein found in wheat flour that allows the dough to rise.

**Glutenin:** Gluten is broken up into two parts; this is the insoluble part.

**Gluten strands:** Cross links formed by kneading the dough. The gluten strands affect the crumb or texture/chewiness of the bread.

**Gliadin:** Gluten is broken up into two parts; this is the soluble part.

**Kneading:** A process by which the dough is mixed, folded, and pressed in a continuous motion to create the gluten strand networks that are needed for the dough to rise.

**Lean bread:** Breads that are made of mainly basic ingredients (flour, water, yeast), without added fats and sugars.

**Levains:** Preferments that use wild yeast as opposed to commercial yeast.

**Liquid starters:** A type of preferment that has a higher hydration percentage than stiff/dry starter to create a wetter, softer mixture.

**Mise en place:** A French saying, meaning to "put everything in its place." This is the first step in the baking process; it calls for the baker to set up all of his or her ingredients and tools prior to beginning the work.

**Oven spring:** The term used to describe the final rise that happens to the bread inside the oven.

**Pâte Fermentée:** The French term for a preferment that uses a portion of old dough as starter in a new batch.

**Peel:** A wide, flat, wooden board with a long handle that is used to slide breads into a hot oven.

**Poolish:** A type of liquid preferment that is made from equal parts water and flour, plus yeast.

**Preferments:** Live, active yeast cultures that are added to dough to give bread more complex flavors.

**Proofing:** The term used to describe the dough left out to rise after it has been shaped.

**Resting:** The term used to describe the dough left out to rise after mixing it but before shaping it.

**Stiff starters:** A type of preferment that has a lower hydration percentage than liquid starters to create a drier, harder mixture.

# INDEX

final dough temperature,
49
in France, 210
hand mixing, 44–45
ingredient sequence in,
46
salt and, 48
stand mixing, 44–45
water in, 46–47
wine starter, 109
moisture. *See also* water
creating steam, 74
hard grains and, 46
round shapes and, 59
salt and, 48
the mother. *See* wine starter
Multigrain Bread, 121

National Sustainable
Information Service, 97
New York, Lower East Side,
16–17
New York Rye Bread, 93, 124
NOFA. *See* Northeast Organic
Farming Association
North Country Mills, 82,
99–101
Northeast Organic Farming
Association (NOFA), 96

Olive Bread, 21, 134
olives, 21
Onion Pockets, 162
Organic Consumers
Association, 97
organic eggs, 96
organic flour, 89
Orwashers Bakery, 19

alliances for, 22
bread by the pound at, 18
consistency at, 20–21, 26
history and, 10, 12,
16–18
as home, 18
immigrants and, 16–17
local ingredients for, 21,
82, 85, 96–97, 99,
101–102
menu at, 21
quality and, 12–13
quantity at, 22
shop, 16
starters at, 21
oven spring, 203
oven thermometer, 39, 72
ovens
hot spots, 38, 72
rising in, 59, 74, 92, 203
too low temperatures in,
72
oxygenation, 50

paddle attachment, for stand
mixers, 37
pans, 41, 59, 202
pastry wheel cutter, 41
pâte fermentée, 107
peels, 41
pizza stone (baking stone), 41
pizza wheel, 41
plain flour, 90
poolish, 107
Potato Burger Buns, 159
potato flour, 95
potatoes, 95
preferments, 104

activity of, 201
additional, 112–113
smell of, 201
water and, 47
presoaking
for hard grains, 46
rye, 93
production, 10
proofing, 70, 71, 204
protein, 47, 86, 94. *See also*
*specific flour types; specific*
*wheat types*
Pullman Bread, 29, 59, 64
Pullman Palace Car Company,
59
Pumpernickel Bread, 30, 93,
127
pumpernickel flour, 93
Pumpernickel Rolls, 168
Pumpkin Bread, 146
punching down (degassing),
52

raisins, 127, 143, 150, 153
Cinnamon Raisin Bread,
144
rapid-rise (instant) yeast, 106
ratios, measurement, 42–43
recipes, reading, 34
refrigerator
bread staleness from, 79
wine starter in, 111
resting dough
in bread baking, 56–57,
210
final state of, 57, 210
in France, 210
gluten and, 56

# ACKNOWLEDGEMENTS

---

I want to sincerely thank everyone who helped bring this book to life.

To the entire Orwashers team: you are an integral part of this business.
The pride you take in the craft of bread-making is evident in every bite. This tireless care,
commitment and professionalism has enabled us to grow and thrive.
Thank you.

I would like to thank my Production Supervisor, Mario, in particular. Without his
dedication and talent, we simply could not have come this far.

Also, heartfelt thanks to my manager, Jessica, for helping me gather and organize my
thoughts during the book writing process. What we do here is so instinctual, I forget
sometimes how many steps it takes to make a great loaf of bread.

I would also like to acknowledge some the people who have enriched both my life and
my business. A. Spinner, S. Kaplan, J. Shaub, Christina, and Alexis, thank you for your
guidance, humor, friendship and encouragement

Lastly and most importantly I want to thank Paula, Ben and Ava.
Their love and support inspires and feeds me.
Love you all.